the DREAM JOURNAL

The Dream Journal
Copyright © 2023 Benjamin Armstrong

All rights reserved. No part of *The Dream Journal* may be reproduced, stored in a retrieval system, or transmitted, in any form or in any means—electronic, mechanical, photocopying, recording or otherwise—in any form without permission. Thank you for buying an authorized edition of this book and for complying with copyright laws.

Scripture quotations marked (NIV) are taken from the Holy Bible, New International Version®, NIV®. Copyright © 1973, 1978, 1984, 2011 by Biblica, Inc.™ Used by permission of Zondervan. All rights reserved worldwide.

Scripture quotations marked (NASB®) are taken from the Holy Bible, New American Standard Bible®, Copyright © 1960, 1971, 1977, 1995, 2020 by The Lockman Foundation. Used by permission. All rights reserved.

ISBN: 979-8-9878024-0-3

THIS JOURNAL BELONGS TO:

_____

I want to dedicate this journal to my family—first, to my incredible wife, Heather, for her belief in me and her heart to steward our family's dreams. To my children, Conner, Kira, and Madison: your love and value for the language of dreams astounds me and provokes me to pursue God even more in the realm of dreams and interpretation. May this journal be a tool to connect us more as a family—not just to each other, but also to the future generations of Armstrongs we have yet to meet. Finally, to all the dreamers out there who know that dreams are treasures to be mined and discovered: thank you! Without you, this journal would not exist.

Foreword

Dreams are not simply subconscious rumblings or futile fantasies. Rather, all throughout history we have seen dreams shift the course of events, save nations, and influence generations. Often they are the very tool that God uses to cut through the chaos and whisper to the hearts of people, passing them the key to unlock miracles, strategies, and solutions to waking-life problems.

Hearing from God through dreams and interpreting those messages is not a gift reserved for elite prophets and full-time ministers, apostles, or gifted individuals in the prophetic department of a church. We could all walk in greater revelation, understanding, and supernatural strategy for our lives if we paid more attention to our dreams. The truth is that whatever you value will increase in your life. In the pages of the journal you are about to read, Ben brilliantly shares a process for stewarding dreams that will inspire you to greater depths of encountering the heart of God as you sleep and launch you into discovering the destiny that is written in the fine lines of your dreams.

Job 33:14–18 (NIV) says: "For God does speak—now one way, now another—though no one perceives it. In a dream, in a vision of the night, when deep sleep falls on people as they slumber in their beds, he may speak in their ears and terrify them with warnings, to turn them from wrongdoing and keep them from pride, to preserve them from the pit, their lives from perishing by the sword."

Did you catch that? God doesn't just give us insights into the unseen realm through dreams; He also uses them to change our attitudes! Just as a surgeon waits until the patient is unconscious before performing an operation, if our souls are resisting the Lord, He waits until we are asleep, and then changes our hearts through visions of the night. Ben often says, "Dreams are not second-class encounters with God. They are vitally important to our personal lives and to what God wants to accomplish on the earth."

This is a powerful reminder that dreams are a catalyst to bring us into relationship with the Giver, to transform our hearts, and to influence the world around us. As you begin to steward your dreams on the pages of this journal, you will be filled with faith for the God of the universe to meet with you and minister to you in your sleep.

KRIS VALLOTTON

SENIOR ASSOCIATE LEADER, BETHEL CHURCH, REDDING, CA
COFOUNDER OF BETHEL SCHOOL OF SUPERNATURAL MINISTRY
AUTHOR OF FIFTEEN BOOKS, INCLUDING *THE SUPERNATURAL WAYS OF ROYALTY* AND *UPRISING*

Welcome

This journal is a "dream" come true for me and has truly been years in the making. I am beyond excited to share it with you.

We spend a third of our lives asleep. By the time we are sixty years old, we will have slept approximately twenty years. This is a cycle of rest, renewal, and revelation initiated by our Creator to enrich our lives with greater levels of connection and wisdom. I hope that as you engage with this tool, you will discover the wealth God has hidden in the night season for you.

May this journal, and possibly many more that you choose to keep in the future, become part of the chronicle of your life—a treasure worth passing down through the generations. Like Abraham, Isaac, Jacob, and Joseph, we are a generation of dreamers who are creating a heritage of connection with God through dreams, visions, and waking encounters. I have found that as we steward the dreams we receive, we step into the fullness of what God intends for our lives.

Thank you for choosing *The Dream Journal*.

BENJAMIN ARMSTRONG

How We Came Up with the Template

I have been using a form of this journaling style for more than fifteen years. It began with the simple habit of recording my dreams and then asking myself and God pointed and practical questions about them, like: *Is this dream about me or someone else? When did the dream come, and is it connected to an issue or experience in my life? How did I feel in the dream?*

I have always been a visual person (and someone I would consider to be pretty creative). The way my mind operates is not always linear (e.g., 1, 2, 3, 4). At times it moves more in circles or figure eights, so when I began mapping my dreams, I would use circles connected by lines. I would put the main focus in the center and any subfocuses in circles around it, thereby keeping the subfocuses connected to the main focus.

Another way to picture this is a honeycomb cluster—an image overflowing with prophetic symbolism. Throughout history, honey has been a treasured commodity. The Promised Land that God gave the Hebrews after they crossed the Red Sea was said to be "a land flowing with milk and honey" (Deuteronomy 26:9 NIV).

Our dreams should have this same kind of value. As we unpack these honeycombs, we will discover that they are filled with the golden, sweet nectar of God's wisdom and solutions. They are also incubators for new life.

Although we could go into great depth on the how-tos of interpreting a dream, I won't do that in these pages; that will be the goal of my future dream interpretation book. The goal of *The Dream Journal* is to introduce you to the language of dreams and the adventure of discovery. Just as it can be a struggle to learn a new language, the practice of journaling and interpretation will take some work. However, with continual practice we can train ourselves in the language of dreams, visions, the prophetic, and encounters, as all of these may have components of metaphoric or parabolic language. Just as consistency with lifting weights causes our muscles to grow, the consistency of practicing the interpretive process will mature our ability to think in the language of dreams.

I believe that as you engage with this journal, you will also begin to "taste and see" (Psalm 34:8 NIV) God's goodness revealed in the mysterious and intimate language of dreams.

The Main Types of Dreams

Dreams are a filter for information. Humans are made up of body, soul, and spirit. As triune beings, we receive information in dreams from these three sources. There are body dreams, soul dreams, and two kinds of spiritual dreams: demonically inspired and God-inspired dreams. Consequently, recognizing the source of the dream will help the dreamer and interpreter more accurately interpret the wisdom potentially available.

Dreams are unique experiences, and it's possible for multiple sources of influence to show up in a single dream. One could have a dream in which the information presented may speak about something that is not only soul-based, but could also include components connected to the body or spirit, and perhaps even both.

Just as we go through our days with our body, soul, and spirit being fully integrated into one another, our dreams can also be alive in one or all of the four main types of dreams.

Let's unpack some examples of each type so that we can better identify them.

⚡ BODY DREAMS

Body dreams can be connected to physical conditions, such as our diets, hormones, or chemicals that could be natural, synthetic, or drug- or alcohol-induced. For example, I've had one body dream many times with small differences in the details: I dream I've lost an arm in some kind of battle or accident. I wake up in a panic, only to realize I have slept on my arm wrong and cut off the circulation to it. This is a simple example of a condition in my body affecting my dreams. My mind is saying, "I can't find my arm!"

Another body dream I have had in the past also had soul-based elements: I was stressed out in my dream, and as a result of the stress, I got a cold sore on my mouth. I woke from the dream with information about both my body (cold sore) and my soul (stress). I had this dream multiple times, and if I didn't deal with the problem in my soul (stress), I found I did get a cold sore soon after. The wisdom released in a simple dream like this was that my unhealthy soul condition was about to have effects on my body.

Many times, our body dreams can be connected to medication we may be taking, or maybe from having had too many drinks at dinner. Awareness and honesty with oneself is vital to accurately interpret dreams and recognize their source.

Over my twenty-plus years of interpretation, and fifteen years of training others to interpret dreams, many people have told me about having specific dreams related to physical conditions in their bodies and thereafter seeing their doctor, only to find out that the information within the dream was accurate. The wisdom released in the dreams helped spur the visit to the doctor, which in turn led to the early discovery and treatment of those conditions. However, there is also another side to this type of dream, because they are not always literal. A dream about someone having a tumor or dying could be connected not to a physical condition, but rather to some kind of other issue such as the end of a season in life, the end of a job, or a negative or cancerous relationship.

The first thing I coach people to do when interpreting a body dream is to visit their doctor. If the dream was not literal, they will discover that quickly without introducing unnecessary fear and anxiety into their life. The second thing I coach them in is the concept of submitting their dreams to a healthy community that knows and values them. You won't believe how quickly this one step helps individuals recognize the dreams' sources and the potential connection to issues or situations in their lives.

⚡ SOUL DREAMS

Most of the thousands of individuals I have coached in dream interpretation have had a few different dreams that speak to soul-based issues connected to their mind, will, desires, and emotions. An example would be a dream in which the dreamer is falling, only to wake up with an extreme feeling of fear or panic. Many times, this type of dream is directly connected to an issue or experience in which the dreamer feels out of control. Another, less extreme version of this is one in which the dreamer is back at school taking a test for which he or she is unprepared, or there is a job he or she is trying to do but the right tools are unavailable. This could also indicate a feeling of being out of control or unprepared for an assignment or deadline at work.

In 2018, a woman told me about a recurring soul-based dream that she was having with a few variations. She was at her university graduation ceremony. Just as she was about to cross the stage to receive her diploma, someone stepped up to stop her, saying she was one credit short of being able to graduate.

This dream and variations of it had been periodic indications that the woman suffered from an overwhelming drive for perfection, accompanied by the sense of never being able to attain it. She knew in some way she would always miss at least one thing that would keep her from the promotions she so desperately desired.

We spent time replacing the lie that if she was not perfect, she would miss out on her potential future. We connected with the Holy Spirit and asked for the truth to replace that lie. The truth He gave was that she could operate in the spirit of excellence: "Whatever you do, work at it with all your heart, as working for the Lord, not for humans" (Colossians 3:23 NIV). The Holy Spirit told her, "You do your best, and I will cover the rest."

It is beautiful to see what the Lord can do when we take soul-based issues revealed in our dreams to Him. His grace uncovers those things concealed in our souls so that we can connect with Him over those matters that concern us. "Cast all your anxiety on him because he cares for you." (1 Peter 5:7 NIV) Soul-based dreams are a powerful source of self-awareness and self-diagnosis. These types of dreams are not always to be ignored or cast aside. They can lead us into an incredible connection with God.

However, we do need to be careful not to think that all dreams have their source in God just because we have a relationship with Him.

⚡ DEMONIC DREAMS

The spirit realm of dreams is often ignored or outright dismissed by most traditional psychologists. This approach to dream interpretation inevitably excludes between one-third and half of the potential meanings and sources a dream may have. Remember, one of our primary anchors for accurate dream interpretation is found in Scripture. Genesis 40:8 (NIV) says, "Do not interpretations belong to God?" Ignoring the One who formed us with a need for rest and intimacy with Him, as well as meeting that need by creating the night season and dreams, is to ignore the One who holds accurate interpretation. Relegating the potential wisdom of dream interpretation to man alone excludes the true Source of all wisdom. While interpreting dreams, I personally have a foundational understanding that I cannot fail in what may seem impossible when I am connected to the Source of all wisdom.

Both demonic dreams and God dreams can be put into the category of spiritual dreams.

Scripture tells us, "Yes, this is what the Lord Almighty, the God of Israel, says: 'Do not let the prophets and diviners among you deceive you. Do not listen to the dreams you encourage them to have" (Jeremiah 29:8 NIV).

Jude explains it this way: "Yet in the same way these men, also by dreaming, defile the flesh, and reject authority, and revile angelic majesties" (Jude 1:8 NASB).

The devil and his minions have long sought to counterfeit and hijack all that God Himself intended for our benefit and our connection with Him. This is also true of our dream life. John 10:10 (NIV) says, "The thief comes only to steal and kill and destroy; I have come that they may have life, and have life to the full." We can be sure that in any area where God has come to create life and the fullness of it, the enemy will try to bring perversion, fear, and death.

For too long, the night season has been relegated to the enemy. Many times, what we feed our souls can open doors to fear, hatred, unforgiveness, sexual sin, and the occult or witchcraft. These doors automatically give the enemy free access to influence us, both while we are awake and asleep.

If one feeds on a diet of horror movies, he or she has opened the door of fear in their life. This in turn can open someone up to the influence of the enemy in their dreams.

The same is true with the epidemic of pornography in our society today. The constant bombardment of perversion strips from us our true identity and leads to depravity, chaos, and confusion. Over time, our sense of morality collapses, and if not reversed, epigenetics tells us that this will have negative effects on our psyches and our society as a whole. Meanwhile, the constant spiritual attack shows up in our dreams, with the enemy slowly eroding our connection to our Creator and increasing our body, soul, and spirit ties to the very thing that seeks to destroy us completely.

You may be thinking, "Ben, this sounds so intense." And my response would be, "Yes, it is intense." But if the enemy can do this over time through either our knowing or unknowing partnership, what can God do with our willing partnership? The answer to this question lies at the basis of our pursuit of dreams and dream interpretation, regardless of their source.

Let's look at an example of a demonic dream:

Some years ago, I had a dream suffused with the feeling of an apocalypse. There was twisted metal, rubble from destroyed buildings, fire, and smoke everywhere. A group of my friends and acquaintances was there, and as we were walking through this scene, vampires were going around biting people who became vampires as well. (Note: I had not watched vampire movies, so I had not been feeding my soul this type of thing and had not opened any doors.) My friends were beginning to freak out. I said to them, "Don't look at them! Close your eyes. If you don't look at them, they can't bite you." Then I woke up.

The great thing about a relationship with God is that even demonically inspired dreams can lead us back into connection with Him. If we respond correctly, these dreams can be an invitation to dialogue with God, or even become intercessory prayer. Joseph declared, "As for you, you meant evil against me, but God meant it for good in order to bring about this present result, to preserve many people alive" (Genesis 50:20 NASB).

As I woke from this particular demonically inspired dream, God unpacked the plans of the enemy for me. "All spiritual realms thrive on attention," He said. "We empower whatever realm we give attention to. What realm are you giving your attention to?" In 1 Thessalonians 5:19–22 (NIV) we are warned about this: "Do not put out the Spirit's fire; do not treat prophecies with contempt. Test everything. Hold on to the good. Avoid every kind of evil." Our job is to look for and hold on to the good and avoid the evil.

The Apostle Paul gives us these instructions in the following passage: "Finally, brethren, whatever is true, whatever is honorable, whatever is right, whatever is pure, whatever is lovely, whatever is of good repute, if there is any excellence and if anything worthy of praise, dwell on these things" (Philippians 4:8 NASB).

These are the things which deserve our focus.

If someone has knowingly or unwittingly opened a door to the demonic, the solution is repentance. "Lord, forgive me for partnering with …" (fill in the blank with which you have partnered). "What new truth do You have for me in exchange for this?" I like to activate the new truth that God has for the individual by asking them to connect with the Holy Spirit and ask, "What is one thing I can physically do on a daily basis to partner with this truth?"

⚡ GOD DREAMS

Spiritual dreams that come from God as the source should be our primary pursuit in the dream realm. God dreams are just that—dreams inspired by God. The purpose of a God dream can include:

- Revealing your calling
- Revealing your destiny
- Edification
- Exhortation
- Revelation of God
- Revelation of Scripture

- Comfort
- Correction
- Direction
- Warning
- Instruction
- Wisdom
- Cleansing
- Revealing the heart
- Spiritual warfare
- Creative solutions
- Impartation
- Intercession
- Healing
- Courage
- Strength
- Word of knowledge
- Prophetic understanding
- Deliverance
- Encounter

This is not an exhaustive list, but it is a good road map for beginning the journey of recognizing God as a potential source of your dreams.

God is all about intimacy. He will use dreams to draw you close to Him and initiate a hunger for seeking Him. Genesis 40:8 (NIV) says, "Do not interpretations belong to God?" Most of our dreams will be symbolic and need interpretation. The questions a dream initiates are invitations to a conversation with the One who is pursuing a deep relationship with us. Genesis 41:16 (NIV) reveals Joseph's acknowledgement: "I cannot do it… but God will give Pharaoh the answer he desires."

It is important to remember that God wants us to understand Him. The Lord is the giver and the interpreter of dreams. In Daniel 2, we read about a dream King Nebuchadnezzar had. It was pretty complex and every part of it was symbolic. Interpreting it required supernatural revelation. Nebuchadnezzar's response in Daniel 2:47 (NIV) confirms: "Surely your God is the God of gods and the Lord of kings and a revealer of mysteries, for you were able to reveal this mystery." A difficult dream is an invitation to an encounter with the God of all mysteries!

In this process we must remember that God's mysteries are not hidden *from* us, but rather hidden *for* us. "It is the glory of God to conceal a matter; to search out a matter is the glory of kings." (Proverbs 25:2 NIV)

God dreams have some distinguishing characteristics and can include the following:

SCRIPTURE RESONANCE

God dreams always align with the Word of God. The dream will resonate with the character and nature of God as revealed in Scripture. Therefore, it is important to contextualize the dream with Scripture.

HOLY SPIRIT

The Holy Spirit is our Guide, Teacher, and Counselor. He will affirm the dream through signs, repetition, and peace that will point to its meaning. He may even give you different forms of the same dream over time. The Apostle Paul emphasized this by stating: "The Spirit himself testifies with our spirit that we are God's children" (Romans 8:16 NIV). Spirit-to-spirit resonance will indicate the source.

COMMUNITY AFFIRMATION

Community consists of your friends and family members who share your values as well as the leaders and authority figures in your life—people you trust more than yourself. Submit the dream to them for evaluation and affirmation of the source. Our community usually knows us best. They know many of our life experiences, aspirations, and needs, and they have a great grid for determining whether the dream comes from God or our own mind, will, or emotions.

FRUIT

God dreams will always produce lasting fruit, such as transformation, identity, wisdom, faith, healing, counsel, freedom, warnings, solutions, or inventions, just to name a few.

TIME

Time is the great revealer of a dream's source. If you are not sure if it came from God, wait on the Lord. Many dreams may take some time to process. God loves the process and the conversation that a dream creates with Him! Interpreting the first dream may take a relatively long time, but as we steward the process, we will become more proficient at it.

In April 2022, I had a God dream while heading to Lubbock, Texas for a ministry trip. I dreamed I was driving with Bill Johnson down a country road. Bill was in the passenger seat; he looked over to me and said, "Ben, did you know that at times people are one measure of gratitude away from their healing or breakthrough?"

Bill Johnson has been my senior pastor for the last forty-four years. He is my spiritual father. At times, God can use a leader in a dream in either a literal or a symbolic way. I believe in this particular dream, Bill not only symbolized a spiritual father giving guidance, but one who has pursued the miraculous through healing for much of his adult life. I also believe he symbolized God the Father—the Healer—teaching me a principle of healing. Gratitude is not the only principle of healing, but it is a part of it and ultimately can be the missing link to a person's breakthrough.

Philippians 4:6 (NIV) tells us to "not be anxious about anything, but in every situation, by prayer and petition, with thanksgiving, present your requests to God."

This dream had scriptural resonance. So the next day, during a time of ministry, we went after healing people's bodies. I asked everyone in the room who needed healing to stand. As they stood, I instructed them to just put thankfulness and gratitude on their lips. After a few minutes of verbally communicating their gratitude to God for all He had done in their past and their present, and thanking Him for all He would do in the future, I had them check out their bodies to see if anything had changed. I asked everyone who felt 80 percent or more improvement to wave both hands. At that moment, more than a dozen people were healed. This led to even more thankfulness and a few more being healed thereafter as well! The community began experiencing the truth of what was released through the dream.

Now there was not only scriptural resonance, but also Holy Spirit affirmation in the power being released for the healing of bodies. The fruit of the dream was a higher value system for a principle of the Kingdom of God and individuals reaping the healing available to them through the heart of gratitude for what Jesus Christ purchased in His body at the cross. The community recognized and affirmed what had been released and experienced. The source of this particular dream took very little time to recognize. I have found that the more I practice these things, the more quickly I am able to identify the type of dream.

The Four Lenses of Interpretation

Recognizing the type of dream we had is vital in identifying the source of the dream and how we should value it. There are multiple lenses through which we can interpret our dreams. Using these lenses will be vital in accurately interpreting your dreams.

⚡ HOLY SPIRIT

Joseph recognized that the true source of interpretation is from God. "'We both had dreams,' they answered, 'but there is no one to interpret them.' Then Joseph said to them, 'Do not interpretations belong to God? Tell me your dreams.'" (Genesis 40:8 NIV)

It is impossible to fully and accurately interpret dreams without the Holy Spirit. Joseph clarified what Pharaoh had heard about him: "Pharaoh said to Joseph, 'I had a dream, and no one can interpret it. But I have heard it said of you that when you hear a dream you can interpret it.' 'I cannot do it,' Joseph replied to Pharaoh, 'but God will give Pharaoh the answer he desires.'" (Genesis 41:15–16 NIV)

Declaring to his court, "Pharaoh asked them, 'Can we find anyone like this man, one in whom is the spirit of God?'" (Genesis 41:38 NIV)

Daniel explained it this way to the king: "No wise man, enchanter, magician or diviner can explain to the king the mystery he has asked about, but there is a God in heaven who reveals mysteries. He has shown King Nebuchadnezzar what will happen in days to come. Your dream and the visions that passed through your mind as you were lying in bed are these ..." (Daniel 2:27–28 NIV)

Nebuchadnezzar attributed revelation to God because of Daniel's esteemed ability: "The king said to Daniel, 'Surely your God is the God of gods and the Lord of kings and a revealer of mysteries, for you were able to reveal this mystery.'" (Daniel 2:47 NIV)

It was reported about Daniel, "There is a man in your kingdom who has the spirit of the holy gods in him. In the time of your father he was found to have insight and intelligence and wisdom like that of the gods. Your father, King Nebuchadnezzar, appointed him chief of the magicians, enchanters, astrologers and diviners." (Daniel 5:11 NIV)

Once again it is stated about Daniel, "I have heard that the spirit of the gods is in you and that you have insight, intelligence and outstanding wisdom." (Daniel 5:14 NIV)

The gift of interpretation, as laid out in 1 Corinthians 12, is one of the gifts of the Holy Spirit. If we intend to be accurate in the interpretation process, then our journey begins with a divine partnership. This partnership recognizes our dependence on the Holy Spirit to mine the mysteries of dreams and visions. Even kings and pharaohs in Scripture, who did not know the God of the Hebrews, knew that the wisdom both Daniel and Joseph displayed was not worldly wisdom, but rather that which flows from the Spirit of God.

Both Daniel and Joseph were deeply submitted to this law of partnership and recognized that their own skill to do what was asked of them was insufficient. They are prime examples of an emphasis on the need for God in the process—and above that, their stories are evidence of the desire for God Himself, His plans, and His purposes for humanity being revealed through the language of dreams. Daniel and Joseph put their own abilities in the right place and humbly glorified God in the process. This display of character moved the leaders they served and eventually led to their promotions. A rightly placed value for the Holy Spirit will in turn bring a rightly placed value for us as individuals.

We find a beautiful illustration of how God guided Jeremiah in the following passage: "The word of the Lord came to me: 'What do you see, Jeremiah?' 'I see the branch of an almond tree,' I replied. The Lord said to me, 'You have seen correctly, for I am watching to see that my word is fulfilled.'" (Jeremiah 1:11-12 NIV)

Through these verses, we see how God presented a play on words in order to train Jeremiah to interpret a message. The word used for an "almond tree" in the Hebrew language is *shaqed*, and the Hebrew word God uses for "watching" is *shoqed*.

⚡ EMOTIONS

We want to pay attention to the emotions that we have within a dream, but not particularly to the emotions we feel when we wake up from that dream. It is vitally important to interpret signs and symbols in the context of the dream, as well as the emotion we were feeling when the color, number, sign, or symbol was presented in the dream.

The primary thing we are looking for is whether emotions are positive or negative in the dream. Was there a feeling of excitement, joy, peace, or contentment? These would be positive emotions. Was there a prevailing feeling of fear, confusion, anxiety, or perversion? These would be negative emotions. While trying to interpret the differing focuses of a dream, we need to keep in mind the emotion we had while experiencing each focus.

For example, take the color green. If I had a negative emotion that I felt during the dream and the color green showed up in the dream, I may interpret green through the overall context of the dream as envy. Have you ever heard the saying "green with envy"? Or maybe you grew up watching

The Incredible Hulk and realize green could symbolize anger. Have you seen the emoji of the green face vomiting? Green could symbolize sickness. Gangrene isn't actually green, but could be a play on words that makes one think of tissue death caused by a lack of blood supply.

Let's look at a few examples of the color green showing up in a positive context. Green can symbolize growth and life, or in the case of stoplights it could indicate that "green means go." Green could speak of eternity, as in the word evergreen, or makes us think of a Christmas tree and think of gifts or family. It could also refer to Ireland (aka "The Emerald Isle").

Naturally, a symbol presented in a dream or vision can have many different potential meanings. This could be either exciting or frustrating, and this is the adventure of learning a new language. I hope that as you honor the emotion of a dream and partner with the Holy Spirit, you will begin to unlock the mysteries that are hidden for you in dreams and visions.

⚡ THE DREAMER'S PERSONAL AND CULTURAL EXPERIENCE

This is one of the first questions I like to ask a person who is seeking help with interpreting a dream: "Do any of the signs, symbols, or focuses mean anything to you?" The important thing to note is that God speaks your language. He knows you, and that includes your cultural background and experiences. God will often use those experiences to define signs and symbols.

Look at the color green again through the lens of cultural experience. If you were raised in the United States, green could symbolize provision or finance because our dollar bills are green.

When I ask dreamers what a symbol means to them, they often say something like, "I don't want to tell you. I want to see what you get."

My response is, "Then I won't interpret your dream." I am not trying to be mean, but the person who received the dream is the most important person in the process; most dreams speak the language that is familiar to the dreamer. I will always check with the dreamer first to see if they already have any feelings, thoughts, or potential interpretations.

We all have different life experiences. On top of that, we all have different cultural backgrounds. Honoring these truths gives us a healthy lens of interpretation.

⚡ THE INTERPRETER'S PERSONAL AND CULTURAL EXPERIENCE

We all have life and cultural experiences. If I am interpreting a dream or a vision, my personal and cultural experiences are the secondary lens I will use rather than the primary. I will first ask the dreamer if a symbol means something to him or her; if it doesn't, I begin to ask myself and the Holy Spirit about potential meanings. I ask the Holy Spirit questions based on the emotion of the dream and what is going on in the dreamer's life because our dreams are often connected to situations that we are facing.

I will then begin to ask specific questions based on my own experiences and see if they connect with the dreamer's life experience. I try not to make definitive statements like, "Green means 'go.'" Instead, I will try to form that thought into a suggestion or question: "Could green mean 'go'?" or "Could green mean new life?" This allows the dreamer to process the details and connect with potential meanings. As the interpreter, I am not just looking for the voice of the Holy Spirit myself, but I am also looking for the dreamer to have Holy Spirit affirmation as well. This could show up as a look of surprise, a statement of "OOOHHH!" or a tear in their eye. Body language in the interpretive process is an important indicator of whether we are on the right track or not.

Now that you have some potential interpretations of the signs and symbols presented in your dream, you may be asking, "How do I transition from a potential interpretation to a chosen interpretation of my dream?" This is when I like to go through a checklist to make sure that I am on track.

- Does this dream and interpretation connect with the context of my waking life?
- Have I communicated with the Holy Spirit for affirmation?
- Have I submitted the potential interpretation of the dream to my friends, family, and leaders who share my values?

Fruit and time are important factors in the recognition of your chosen interpretation. This may be frustrating, but it is sometimes important to sit with your potential interpretation for some time to see if it bears fruit, indicating the correct interpretation.

How to Interact With the Journal

This journal was designed to make it easy for you to connect with God daily through journaling, mapping, interpreting, and applying the wisdom gleaned from your dreams. This will create new habits and values for all dreamers in order to mine the depths of wisdom available to each of us. There are three main components to dream interpretation: revelation, interpretation, and application. Dreams are a language of mystery and intimacy, so just having the dream itself is not enough. Most dreams are not literal, so we need interpretation to go with the revelation. However, if we stop at interpretation and never let the new information be a catalyst for change in our lives, we may miss out on the true riches that lie within the night season in the form of dreams.

CONNECTION: Your journaling begins with connection. In Genesis 40:8 (NIV), Joseph declares to the cupbearer and the baker, "Do not interpretations belong to God?" Likewise, in 1 Corinthians 12:10 (NIV), the Apostle Paul reveals that one of the gifts of the Spirit is "interpretation of tongues" (meaning the interpretation of languages). Connection with the One who is the source of all accurate interpretation is fundamental to this whole process; without it, you have nothing of lasting value. As I often say, "Dreams are God's language of intimacy."

FACETS OF CONNECTION

TITLE: Giving a title to your dream as if it were a book, short story, or movie will help you connect with potential themes within it.

DATE: Write down the date you received the dream. This may reveal a connection to an event, issue, or situation in your waking life that your dream may be addressing.

EMOTION: Recording the main emotion(s) that were prevalent in the dream, specifically whether they were positive or negative, will provide an important lens through which to interpret the main focus and subfocuses presented. It can also reveal the source of the dream, which in turn will give you valuable information about how to apply, steward, or pray into it.

DREAM CONTENT: When recording your dream, aim to be as concise as possible without losing any of the important details. For example, if you saw a vehicle, did you recognize the maker (Toyota, Jaguar, Honda, Ford, Lexus, Cadillac, etc.)? What color was it? Was it a convertible, a truck, a bus, or an SUV? Being concise will help you avoid analysis paralysis.

TYPE(S) OF DREAM: As mentioned previously, there are four main types of dreams. Your dream can be more than one type. When going through your dream, check all the types that apply. You will find this helpful in discerning the source of your dream.

LENSES OF INTERPRETATION: When interpreting your dream, go through each lens of interpretation. It is important to dialogue with the Holy Spirit and recognize any lens of emotion you may be using. Keep both your cultural and life experiences as the dreamer in mind, and also the cultural and life experiences of the interpreter. Being aware of the different lenses of interpretation will create even more clarity when interpreting the dream.

MAPPING (HONEYCOMB): The mapping of the dream starts with identifying its main focus and any subfocuses. Start by placing these focuses into the honeycomb diagram provided in this journal to help you visualize the relationship between the different components of your dream. For example, if you, the dreamer, played an active role in the dream, then that would most likely make you the main focus. Usually, the main focus will be literal and will not need much, if any, interpretation.

Although some dreams can be very long and detailed, try to limit yourself to five to eight subfocuses (or less) per dream to help eliminate the aforementioned analysis paralysis. Subfocuses are generally symbolic and will need interpretation. Using the honeycomb diagram as a visual aid in the dream mapping section of this journal will help you keep the main focus in the middle and subfocuses, with their possible interpretations, in the outer ring.

There may be times when we have multiple scenes or storylines within one dream. We would use the same tools in order to interpret each of the scenes, and it may even be appropriate to use multiple journal entries and mapping sections for each scene.

MAIN FOCUS AND SUBFOCUSES: Within the bottom third of the mapping section of each journal entry, on the left side, we have the main focus and subfocus in descending order. In the main focus area, write the main character of the dream. Often, the dreamer will be the main focus; however, that is not always the case. Below the main focus, include each of the subfocuses.

When bringing down the subfocuses from the honeycomb, try your best to write them in the correct order that they happened in the dream. The chronological order is important for the dreamer in identifying instructions or directions laid out in the dream. The order may also be connected to time periods—days, months or even years. The following passage illustrates this importance: "The seven good cows are seven years, and the seven good heads of grain are seven years; it is one and the same dream. The seven lean, ugly cows that came up afterward are seven years, and so are the seven worthless heads of grain scorched by the east wind: They are seven years of famine." (Genesis 41:26–27 NIV) The number seven was connected to years in this particular case.

Some years ago, I interpreted a dream for a friend of mine who had four consecutive dreams in one night. We discovered, through mapping out each of the dreams independently, that each dream corresponded with a year in his life. The first dream represented his life two and a half years earlier, and lined up with everything that was going on in his life at that time. The second dream represented his life a year and a half earlier. The third dream represented his life six months earlier and spoke about the six months ahead of him. His final dream spoke about the year following that. Keeping the dreams independent and then reconnecting them helped us identify God's hand in his journey through the past, present, and future.

To the right of the main focus and subfocus lines and to the left of the interpretation lines are the words "literal" and "symbolic." Mark "literal" next to the focuses which are literal in meaning and "symbolic" next to those which symbolize something in the dream. These are great visual cues that will train us through repetitive use to regularly ask if something is literal or symbolic. If it is symbolic, then it will need interpretation.

INTERPRETATION: Within the bottom third of the mapping section of each journal entry, on the right side of the page, we have a space for the interpretation of the focus. By using the positive or negative emotions lens, you can now begin to interpret the main focus and the subfocuses you just mapped out. For example, if another individual showed up in the dream, did you know the person? What is their name? What does their name mean? What position do they hold in your life? Are they a friend, a coworker, a boss, or a relative? These details will help you identify what that subfocus symbolizes.

INTERPRETATION SUMMARY: Once you have filled out the Dream Mapping portion of the journal, you will want to make a summary statement of interpretation.

APPLICATION: Ask yourself and God, "What is one thing I can do to practically apply or deal with the revelation I have just received?" Write down your answer and start putting it into practice. There isn't always grace for changing a hundred different things in your life but there is grace to do one thing until it becomes a habit. This stewardship brings about an increase of God's grace to do more things that may have been revealed as action points in the dream.

If negative thoughts or lies are exposed in our dreams, then the first thing we want to do is to exchange that lie for the truth. Ask the Holy Spirit, "What truth do you have for me in place of this lie?" Once you receive the new truth, ask, "If this is true, what is one thing I can physically do to show that I believe it?" This is putting our faith in action, and when we do this we will accelerate into the apprehension of the fulfillment of our dreams and our destinies.

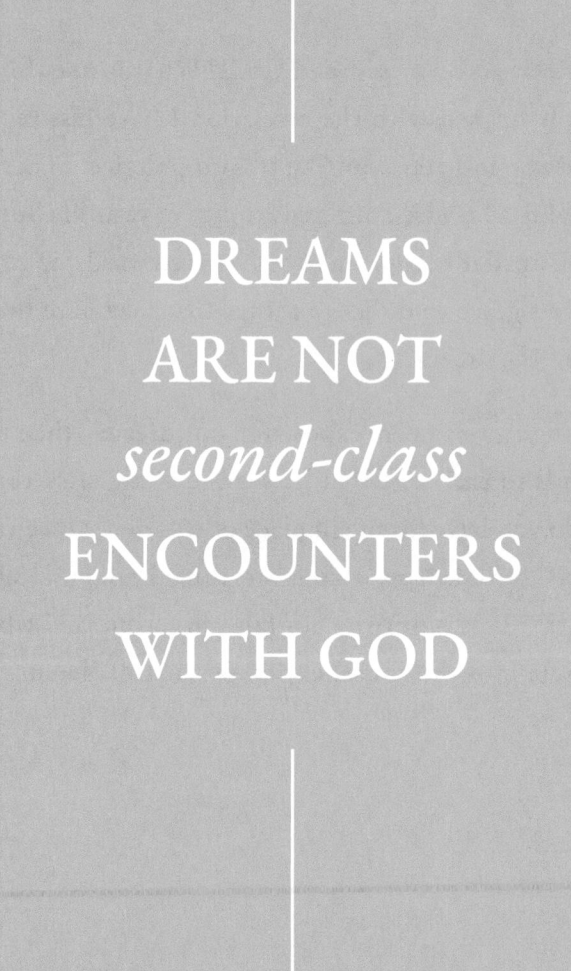

DREAMS ARE NOT *second-class* ENCOUNTERS WITH GOD

The Dream That Changed History
DEVOTIONAL NO. 1

"This is how the birth of Jesus the Messiah came about: His mother Mary was pledged to be married to Joseph, but before they came together, she was found to be pregnant through the Holy Spirit. Because Joseph, her husband, was faithful to the law, and yet did not want to expose her to public disgrace, he had in mind to divorce her quietly. But after he had considered this, an angel of the Lord appeared to him in a dream and said, 'Joseph, son of David, do not be afraid to take Mary home as your wife, because what is conceived in her is from the Holy Spirit. She will give birth to a son, and you are to give him the name Jesus, because he will save his people from their sins.'"

// MATTHEW 1:18–21 (NIV)

One of the greatest events in history, the birth of Jesus, was marked by an angelic encounter. This encounter was unique because the Bible does not just say "an angel of the Lord appeared to Joseph." Scripture is clear about the encounter taking place "in a dream" (Matthew 1:20 NIV). In fact, the first two chapters of the Gospel according to Matthew contain five accounts of dreams that preserved and protected the move of God on the earth. Four of those were dreams Joseph had, and one was a dream the Magi had that saved their lives. Dreams are not second-class encounters with God. They are vitally important to our personal lives and to what God wants to accomplish on the earth.

DEVOTIONAL NOTES

Dream Example

Three Dragons
Dreamer: Conner Armstrong

Dream Title

Three Dragons

DAY OF THE WEEK
S M T W T (F) S

DATE
07 / 17 / 16

PRIMARY EMOTION
(+) / −

DREAM CONTENT

There were three incredible dragons in the dream. First there was a beautiful blue dragon. It wasn't just blue like the blue we have here on Earth—it was a blue like I had never seen before: beautiful, astounding, alive. It must have been a color from Heaven, not from Earth.

The second dragon was just as incredible and breathtaking, but this one was the color green—deep, iridescent, vibrant green like I have never experienced before here on Earth!

The last dragon was even more beautiful and incredible than the first two, if you can believe that. It was a deep red with golden belly scales. The golden belly scales were in the form of a Celtic knot.

He was magnificent! This last dragon was complaining to the other two dragons that he was ugly.

Your sons and daughters will prophesy, your young men will see visions, your old men will dream dreams. (Acts 2:17–18 NIV)

The dragon ran his hand across his belly and said, 'I am so ugly.' The other two dragons, the blue and the green one, said, 'You are crazy, you are the most beautiful dragon we have ever seen!'

Dream Mapping

TYPE(S) OF DREAM *(Check all that apply)*

- ◯ Body Dream
- ✗ Soul Dream
- ◯ Demonic Dream
- ✗ God Dream

LENSES OF INTERPRETATION *(Check once completed)*

- ✗ Holy Spirit
- ✗ Emotion
- ✗ Dreamer's Personal / Cultural Experience
- ✗ Interpreter's Personal / Cultural Experience

MAIN FOCUS	▶	red/gold dragon	▶	LITERAL
SUBFOCUS	▶	blue dragon	▶	LITERAL
SUBFOCUS	▶	green dragon	▶	LITERAL
SUBFOCUS	▶		▶	LITERAL
SUBFOCUS	▶		▶	LITERAL
SUBFOCUS	▶		▶	LITERAL
SUBFOCUS	▶		▶	LITERAL

SUBFOCUS

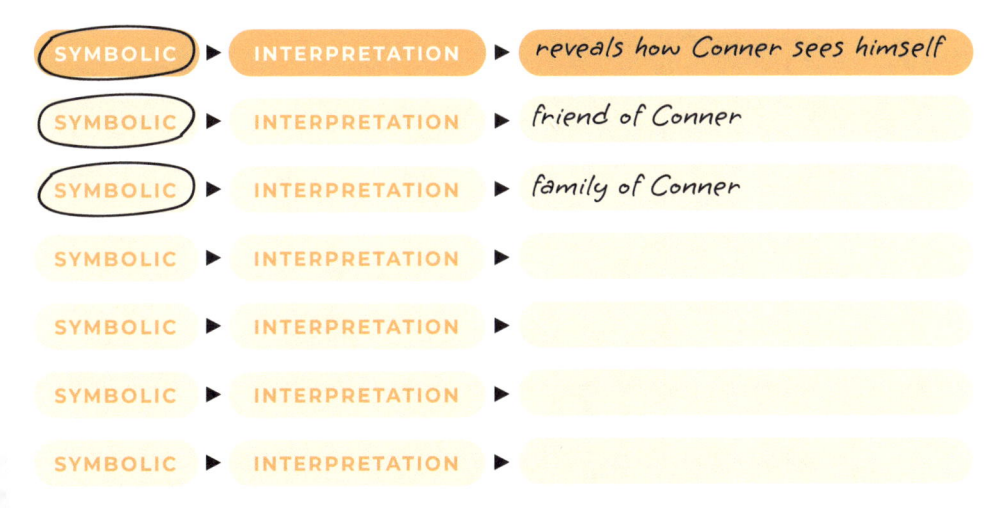

SUBFOCUS
blue dragon

SUBFOCUS
green dragon

MAIN FOCUS
red/gold dragon

SUBFOCUS

SUBFOCUS

SUBFOCUS

(SYMBOLIC) ▶	INTERPRETATION ▶	reveals how Conner sees himself
(SYMBOLIC) ▶	INTERPRETATION ▶	friend of Conner
(SYMBOLIC) ▶	INTERPRETATION ▶	family of Conner
SYMBOLIC ▶	INTERPRETATION ▶	
SYMBOLIC ▶	INTERPRETATION ▶	
SYMBOLIC ▶	INTERPRETATION ▶	
SYMBOLIC ▶	INTERPRETATION ▶	

INTERPRETATION SUMMARY

As Conner was explaining this to me in the hotel room, his sister, Kira, was getting ready in the bathroom, not paying any attention to Conner as he explained the dream. Conner, shirtless, mimicked the red and gold dragons in the dream, looking down and running his hand across his own stomach. "The red dragon is you, Conner, and you don't know how beautiful you are!" Kira yelled from the bathroom. Conner was confronted with an idea rooted in his soul that he was ugly, even though all his friends would tell him otherwise. The dream exposed how far off his way of thinking was and confronted a negative belief system he had about himself. God was faithful to expose the lie he was believing and in turn reveal the truth of his beauty.

APPLICATION

Change the negative self-talk and partner with the truth revealed in the dream by declaring what God thinks and by agreeing with the encouragement of his friends.

Dream Title

Dream Title

DAY OF THE WEEK
S M T W T F S

DATE
/ /

PRIMARY EMOTION
+ / −

DREAM CONTENT

It is the glory of God to conceal a matter,
But the glory of kings is to search out a matter. (Proverbs 25:2 NASB)

Dream Mapping

TYPE(S) OF DREAM *(Check all that apply)*

- Body Dream
- Soul Dream
- Demonic Dream
- God Dream

LENSES OF INTERPRETATION *(Check once completed)*

- Holy Spirit
- Emotion
- Dreamer's Personal / Cultural Experience
- Interpreter's Personal / Cultural Experience

MAIN FOCUS	▶		▶	LITERAL
SUBFOCUS	▶		▶	LITERAL
SUBFOCUS	▶		▶	LITERAL
SUBFOCUS	▶		▶	LITERAL
SUBFOCUS	▶		▶	LITERAL
SUBFOCUS	▶		▶	LITERAL
SUBFOCUS	▶		▶	LITERAL

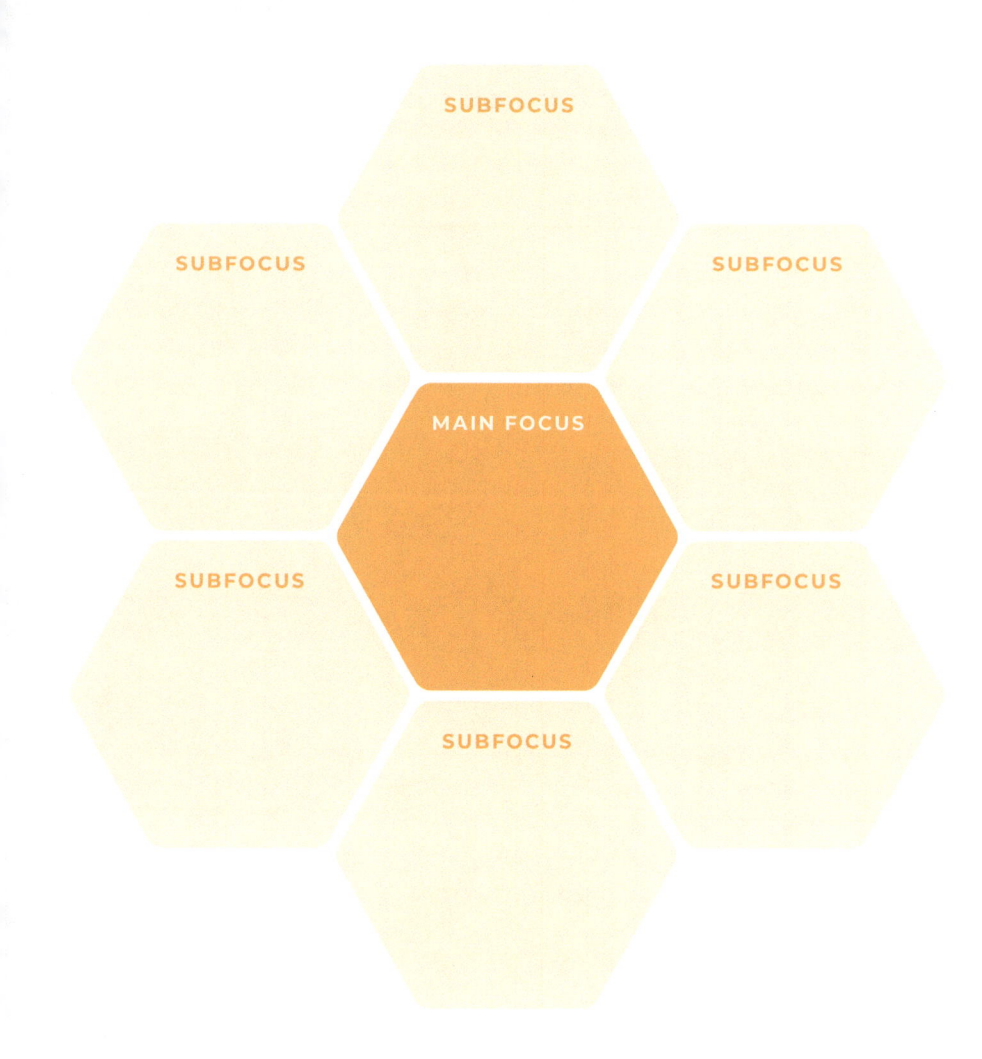

SUBFOCUS

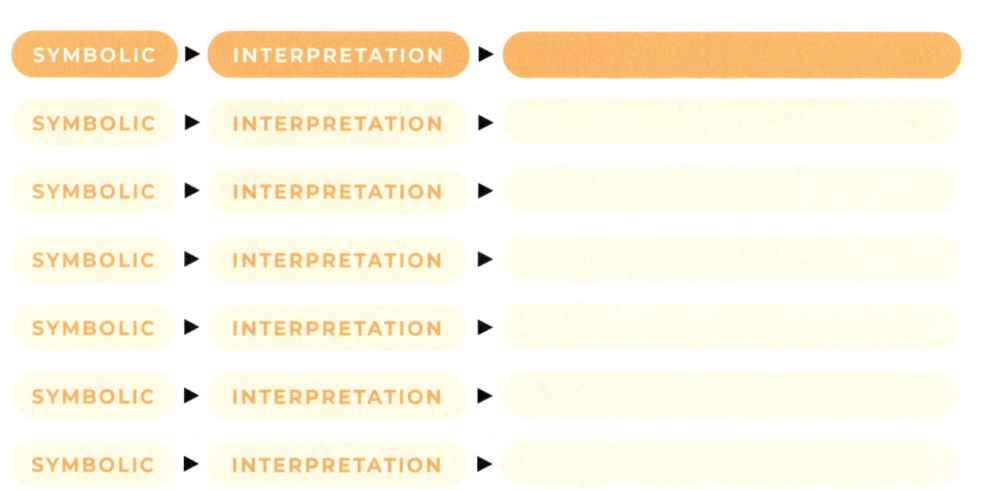

SUBFOCUS

SUBFOCUS

MAIN FOCUS

SUBFOCUS

SUBFOCUS

SUBFOCUS

SYMBOLIC	▶	INTERPRETATION	▶	
SYMBOLIC	▶	INTERPRETATION	▶	
SYMBOLIC	▶	INTERPRETATION	▶	
SYMBOLIC	▶	INTERPRETATION	▶	
SYMBOLIC	▶	INTERPRETATION	▶	
SYMBOLIC	▶	INTERPRETATION	▶	
SYMBOLIC	▶	INTERPRETATION	▶	

INTERPRETATION SUMMARY

APPLICATION

Dream Title

Dream Title

DAY OF THE WEEK	DATE	PRIMARY EMOTION
S M T W T F S	/ /	+ / −

DREAM CONTENT

*The key steps to dream interpretation are revelation,
interpretation, and application.*

Dream Mapping

TYPE(S) OF DREAM *(Check all that apply)*

- Body Dream
- Soul Dream
- Demonic Dream
- God Dream

LENSES OF INTERPRETATION *(Check once completed)*

- Holy Spirit
- Emotion
- Dreamer's Personal / Cultural Experience
- Interpreter's Personal / Cultural Experience

MAIN FOCUS	▶		▶	LITERAL
SUBFOCUS	▶		▶	LITERAL
SUBFOCUS	▶		▶	LITERAL
SUBFOCUS	▶		▶	LITERAL
SUBFOCUS	▶		▶	LITERAL
SUBFOCUS	▶		▶	LITERAL
SUBFOCUS	▶		▶	LITERAL

SUBFOCUS

SUBFOCUS

SUBFOCUS

SUBFOCUS

MAIN FOCUS

SUBFOCUS

SUBFOCUS

SUBFOCUS

SYMBOLIC ▶ INTERPRETATION ▶

SYMBOLIC ▶ INTERPRETATION ▶

SYMBOLIC ▶ INTERPRETATION ▶

SYMBOLIC ▶ INTERPRETATION ▶

SYMBOLIC ▶ INTERPRETATION ▶

SYMBOLIC ▶ INTERPRETATION ▶

SYMBOLIC ▶ INTERPRETATION ▶

INTERPRETATION SUMMARY

APPLICATION

Dream Title

Dream Title

DAY OF THE WEEK	DATE	PRIMARY EMOTION
S M T W T F S	/ /	+ / −

DREAM CONTENT

The wisdom of the ages is stored up for you.

Dream Mapping

TYPE(S) OF DREAM *(Check all that apply)*

- Body Dream
- Soul Dream
- Demonic Dream
- God Dream

LENSES OF INTERPRETATION *(Check once completed)*

- Holy Spirit
- Emotion
- Dreamer's Personal / Cultural Experience
- Interpreter's Personal / Cultural Experience

MAIN FOCUS	▶		▶	LITERAL
SUBFOCUS	▶		▶	LITERAL
SUBFOCUS	▶		▶	LITERAL
SUBFOCUS	▶		▶	LITERAL
SUBFOCUS	▶		▶	LITERAL
SUBFOCUS	▶		▶	LITERAL
SUBFOCUS	▶		▶	LITERAL

SUBFOCUS

SUBFOCUS

SUBFOCUS

MAIN FOCUS

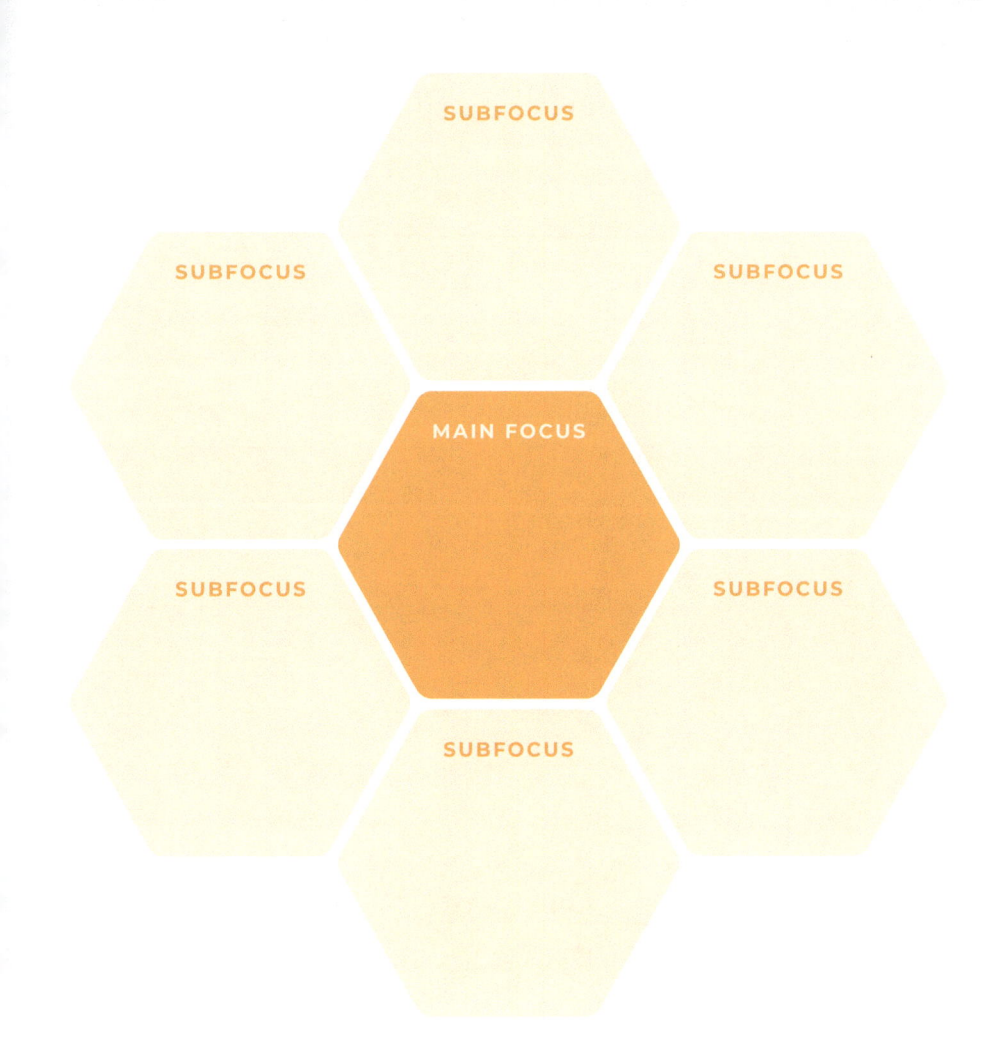

SUBFOCUS

SUBFOCUS

SUBFOCUS

SYMBOLIC	▶	INTERPRETATION	▶	
SYMBOLIC	▶	INTERPRETATION	▶	
SYMBOLIC	▶	INTERPRETATION	▶	
SYMBOLIC	▶	INTERPRETATION	▶	
SYMBOLIC	▶	INTERPRETATION	▶	
SYMBOLIC	▶	INTERPRETATION	▶	
SYMBOLIC	▶	INTERPRETATION	▶	

INTERPRETATION SUMMARY

APPLICATION

Dream Title

Dream Title

DAY OF THE WEEK
S M T W T F S

DATE
/ /

PRIMARY EMOTION
+ / −

DREAM CONTENT

God speaks in metaphors and symbols because He desires a deeper relationship with us, and He knows that this can cause us to dialogue with Him.

Dream Mapping

TYPE(S) OF DREAM *(Check all that apply)*

- Body Dream
- Soul Dream
- Demonic Dream
- God Dream

LENSES OF INTERPRETATION *(Check once completed)*

- Holy Spirit
- Emotion
- Dreamer's Personal / Cultural Experience
- Interpreter's Personal / Cultural Experience

MAIN FOCUS	▶		▶	LITERAL
SUBFOCUS	▶		▶	LITERAL
SUBFOCUS	▶		▶	LITERAL
SUBFOCUS	▶		▶	LITERAL
SUBFOCUS	▶		▶	LITERAL
SUBFOCUS	▶		▶	LITERAL
SUBFOCUS	▶		▶	LITERAL

SUBFOCUS

SUBFOCUS

SUBFOCUS

MAIN FOCUS

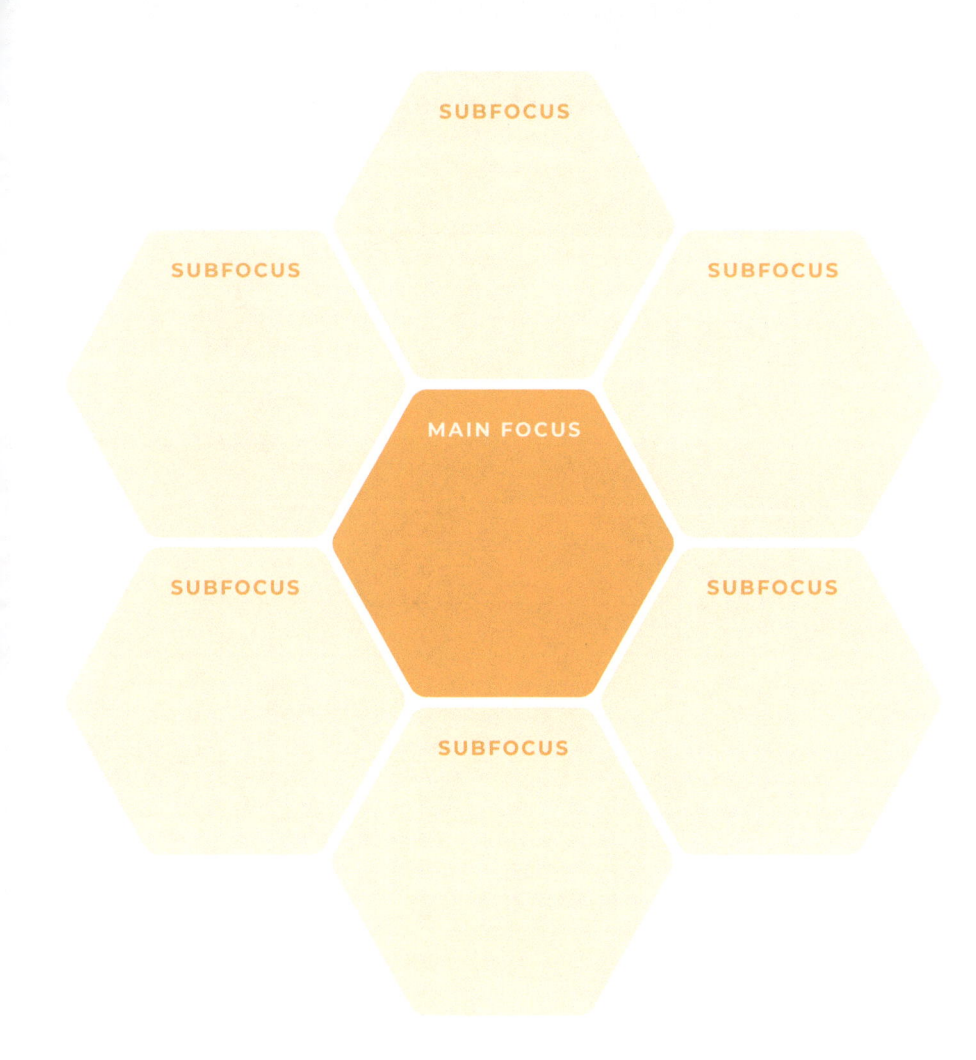

SUBFOCUS

SUBFOCUS

SUBFOCUS

SYMBOLIC	▶	INTERPRETATION	▶	
SYMBOLIC	▶	INTERPRETATION	▶	
SYMBOLIC	▶	INTERPRETATION	▶	
SYMBOLIC	▶	INTERPRETATION	▶	
SYMBOLIC	▶	INTERPRETATION	▶	
SYMBOLIC	▶	INTERPRETATION	▶	
SYMBOLIC	▶	INTERPRETATION	▶	

INTERPRETATION SUMMARY

APPLICATION

Dream Title

Dream Title

DAY OF THE WEEK	DATE	PRIMARY EMOTION
S M T W T F S	/ /	+ / −

DREAM CONTENT

For God does speak—now one way, now another— though no one perceives it. In a dream, in a vision of the night, when deep sleep falls on people as they slumber in their beds. (Job 33:14–15 NIV)

Dream Mapping

TYPE(S) OF DREAM *(Check all that apply)*

- ○ Body Dream
- ○ Soul Dream
- ○ Demonic Dream
- ○ God Dream

LENSES OF INTERPRETATION *(Check once completed)*

- ○ Holy Spirit
- ○ Emotion
- ○ Dreamer's Personal / Cultural Experience
- ○ Interpreter's Personal / Cultural Experience

MAIN FOCUS ▶	▶ LITERAL
SUBFOCUS ▶	▶ LITERAL
SUBFOCUS ▶	▶ LITERAL
SUBFOCUS ▶	▶ LITERAL
SUBFOCUS ▶	▶ LITERAL
SUBFOCUS ▶	▶ LITERAL
SUBFOCUS ▶	▶ LITERAL

SUBFOCUS

SUBFOCUS

SUBFOCUS

MAIN FOCUS

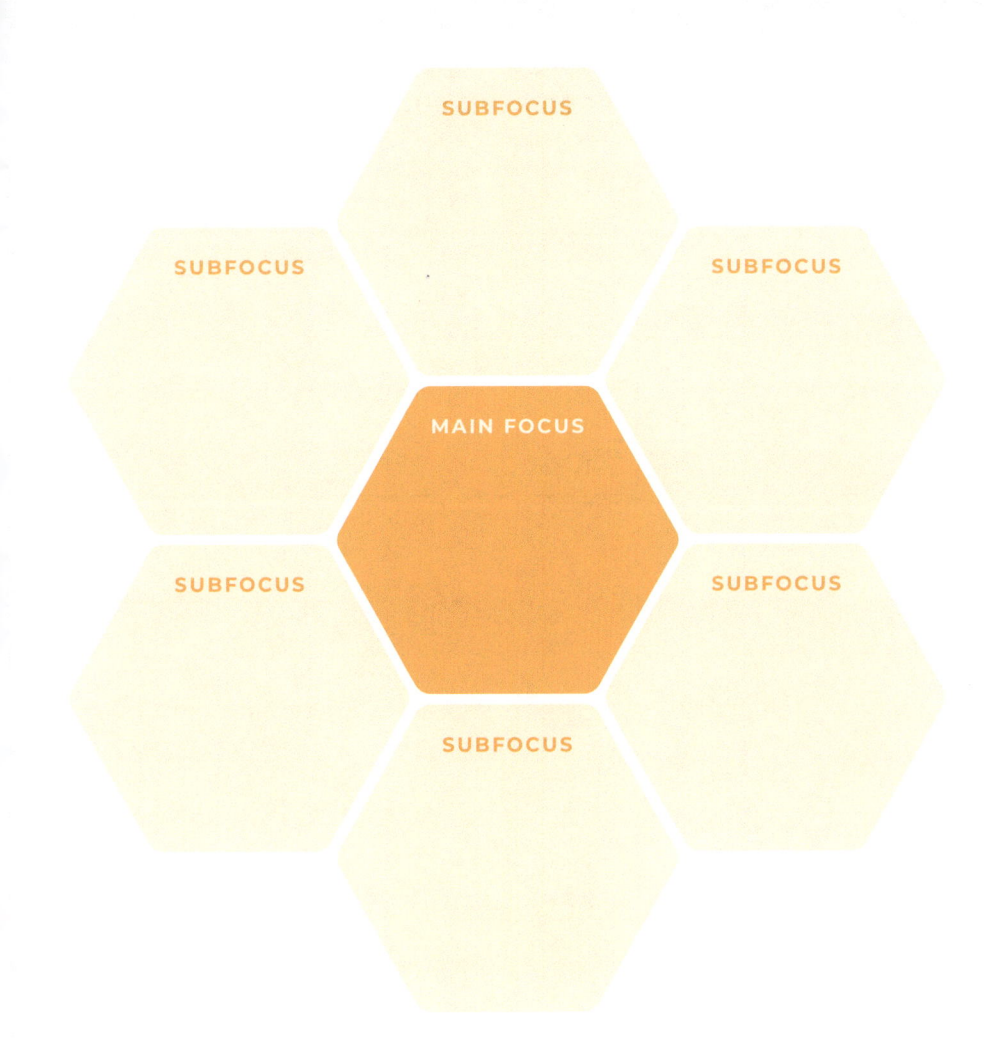

SUBFOCUS

SUBFOCUS

SUBFOCUS

SYMBOLIC	▶	INTERPRETATION	▶	
SYMBOLIC	▶	INTERPRETATION	▶	
SYMBOLIC	▶	INTERPRETATION	▶	
SYMBOLIC	▶	INTERPRETATION	▶	
SYMBOLIC	▶	INTERPRETATION	▶	
SYMBOLIC	▶	INTERPRETATION	▶	
SYMBOLIC	▶	INTERPRETATION	▶	

INTERPRETATION SUMMARY

APPLICATION

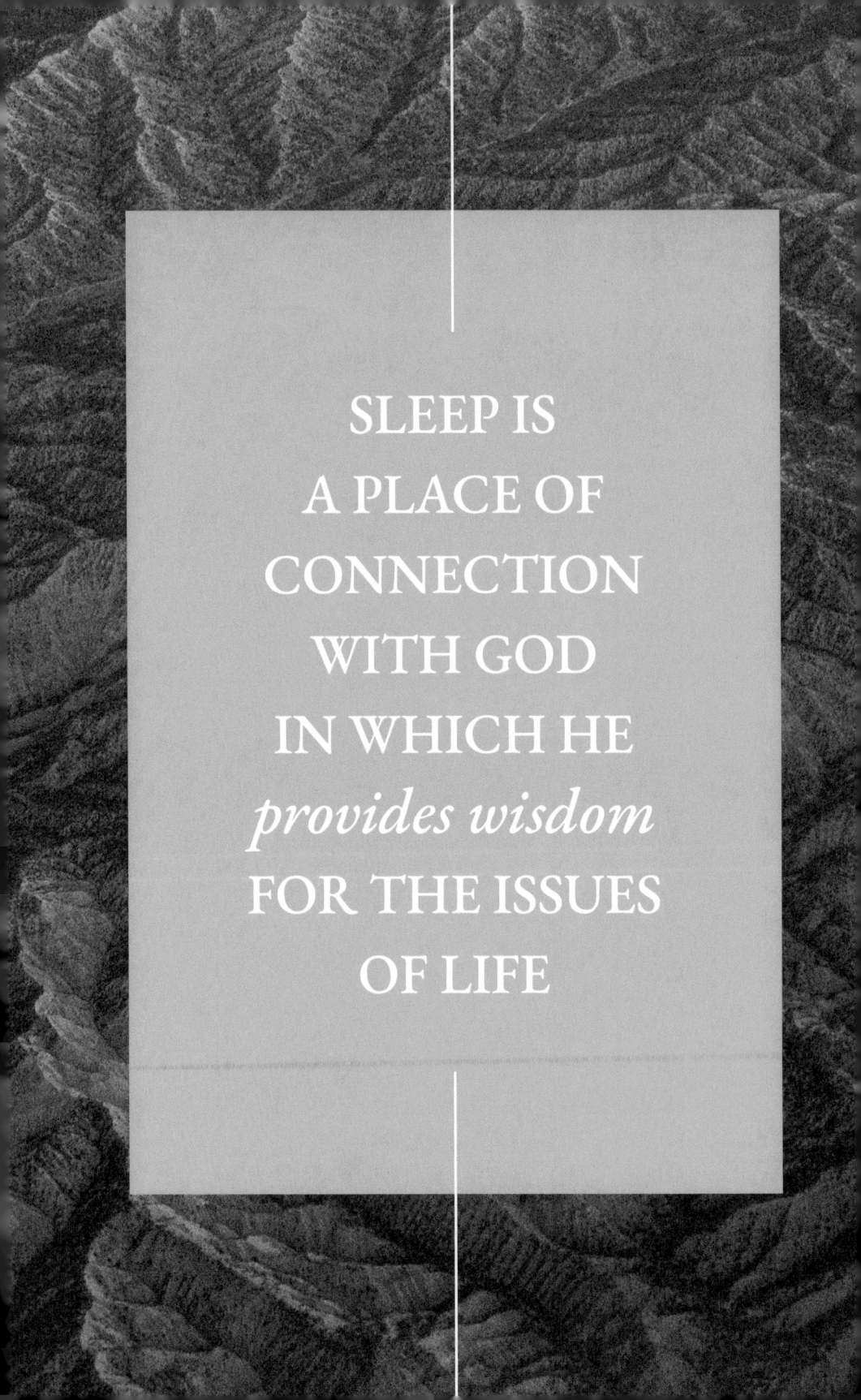

SLEEP IS
A PLACE OF
CONNECTION
WITH GOD
IN WHICH HE
provides wisdom
FOR THE ISSUES
OF LIFE

Resting in God's Promises
DEVOTIONAL NO. 2

Jacob left Beersheba and set out for Haran. When he reached a certain place, he stopped for the night because the sun had set. Taking one of the stones there, he put it under his head and lay down to sleep. He had a dream in which he saw a stairway resting on the earth, with its top reaching to heaven, and the angels of God were ascending and descending on it. There above it stood the Lord, and he said: "I am the Lord, the God of your father Abraham and the God of Isaac. I will give you and your descendants the land on which you are lying. Your descendants will be like the dust of the earth, and you will spread out to the west and to the east, to the north and to the south. All peoples on earth will be blessed through you and your offspring. I am with you and will watch over you wherever you go, and I will bring you back to this land. I will not leave you until I have done what I have promised you." When Jacob awoke from his sleep, he thought, "Surely the Lord is in this place, and I was not aware of it." He was afraid and said, "How awesome is this place! This is none other than the house of God; this is the gate of heaven."

// GENESIS 28:10–17 (NIV)

Jacob, who is running for his life, lays his head on a stone and falls asleep. How many of us have gone to sleep, worn out from the hard issues we are facing? Sometimes we have made a stone (our issue) a pillow. This is what Jacob did, and when he fell asleep, he dreamed of a ladder to Heaven and angels ascending and descending on it. When he woke, he declared, "Surely God was in this place, and I didn't even know it." What issues or hardships are you facing right now? That is where God wants to show up and send you heavenly help and breakthrough.

DEVOTIONAL NOTES

Dream Title

Dream Title

DAY OF THE WEEK
S M T W T F S

DATE
/ /

PRIMARY EMOTION
+ / −

DREAM CONTENT

To these four young men God gave knowledge and understanding of all kinds of literature and learning. And Daniel could understand visions and dreams of all kinds. (Daniel 1:17 NIV)

Dream Mapping

TYPE(S) OF DREAM *(Check all that apply)*

- Body Dream
- Soul Dream
- Demonic Dream
- God Dream

LENSES OF INTERPRETATION *(Check once completed)*

- Holy Spirit
- Emotion
- Dreamer's Personal / Cultural Experience
- Interpreter's Personal / Cultural Experience

MAIN FOCUS	▶		▶	LITERAL
SUBFOCUS	▶		▶	LITERAL
SUBFOCUS	▶		▶	LITERAL
SUBFOCUS	▶		▶	LITERAL
SUBFOCUS	▶		▶	LITERAL
SUBFOCUS	▶		▶	LITERAL
SUBFOCUS	▶		▶	LITERAL

SUBFOCUS

SUBFOCUS

SUBFOCUS

SUBFOCUS

MAIN FOCUS

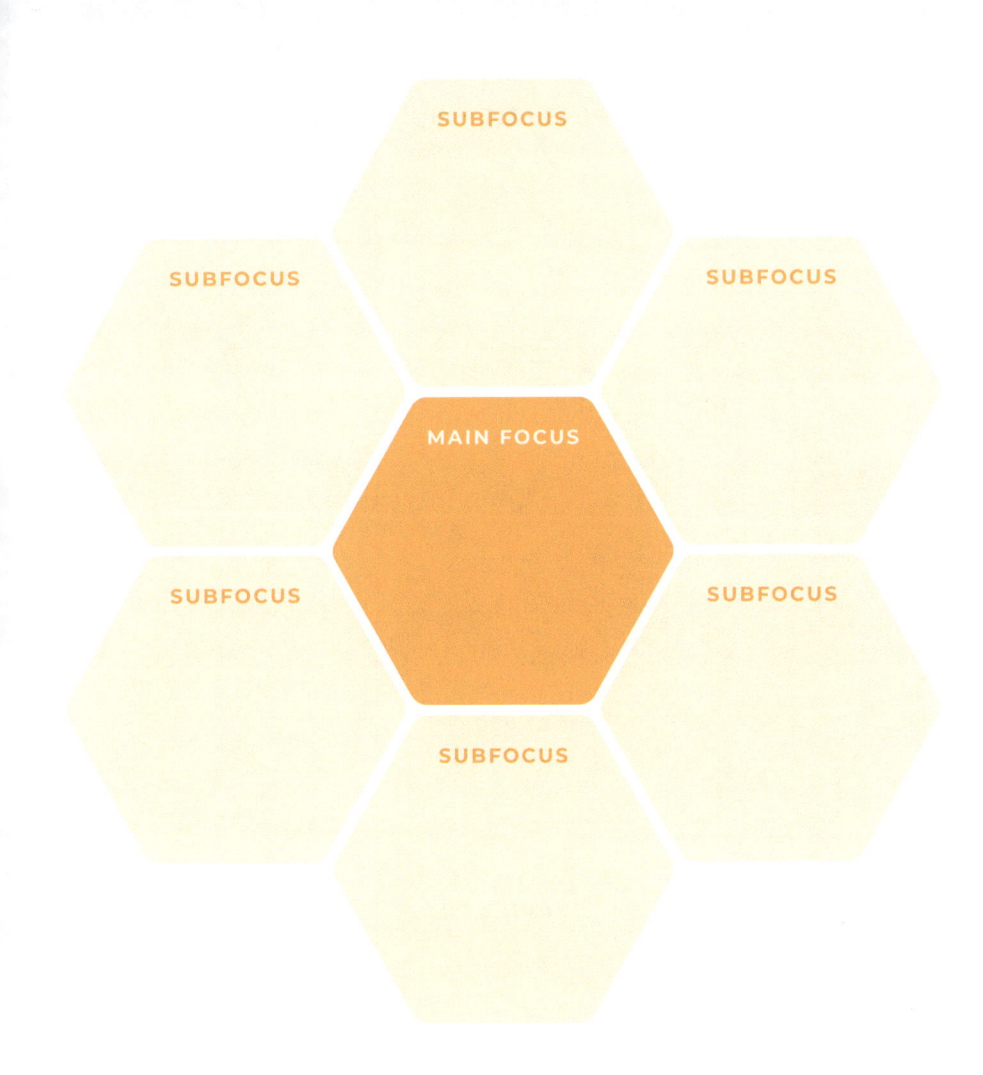

SUBFOCUS

SUBFOCUS

SUBFOCUS

SYMBOLIC	▶	INTERPRETATION	▶	
SYMBOLIC	▶	INTERPRETATION	▶	
SYMBOLIC	▶	INTERPRETATION	▶	
SYMBOLIC	▶	INTERPRETATION	▶	
SYMBOLIC	▶	INTERPRETATION	▶	
SYMBOLIC	▶	INTERPRETATION	▶	
SYMBOLIC	▶	INTERPRETATION	▶	

INTERPRETATION SUMMARY

APPLICATION

Dream Title

Dream Title

DAY OF THE WEEK	DATE	PRIMARY EMOTION
S M T W T F S	/ /	+ / −

DREAM CONTENT

Right interpretation is a matter of connection to the Holy Spirit.

Dream Mapping

TYPE(S) OF DREAM *(Check all that apply)*

- Body Dream
- Soul Dream
- Demonic Dream
- God Dream

LENSES OF INTERPRETATION *(Check once completed)*

- Holy Spirit
- Emotion
- Dreamer's Personal / Cultural Experience
- Interpreter's Personal / Cultural Experience

MAIN FOCUS	▶		▶	LITERAL
SUBFOCUS	▶		▶	LITERAL
SUBFOCUS	▶		▶	LITERAL
SUBFOCUS	▶		▶	LITERAL
SUBFOCUS	▶		▶	LITERAL
SUBFOCUS	▶		▶	LITERAL
SUBFOCUS	▶		▶	LITERAL

SUBFOCUS

SUBFOCUS

SUBFOCUS

MAIN FOCUS

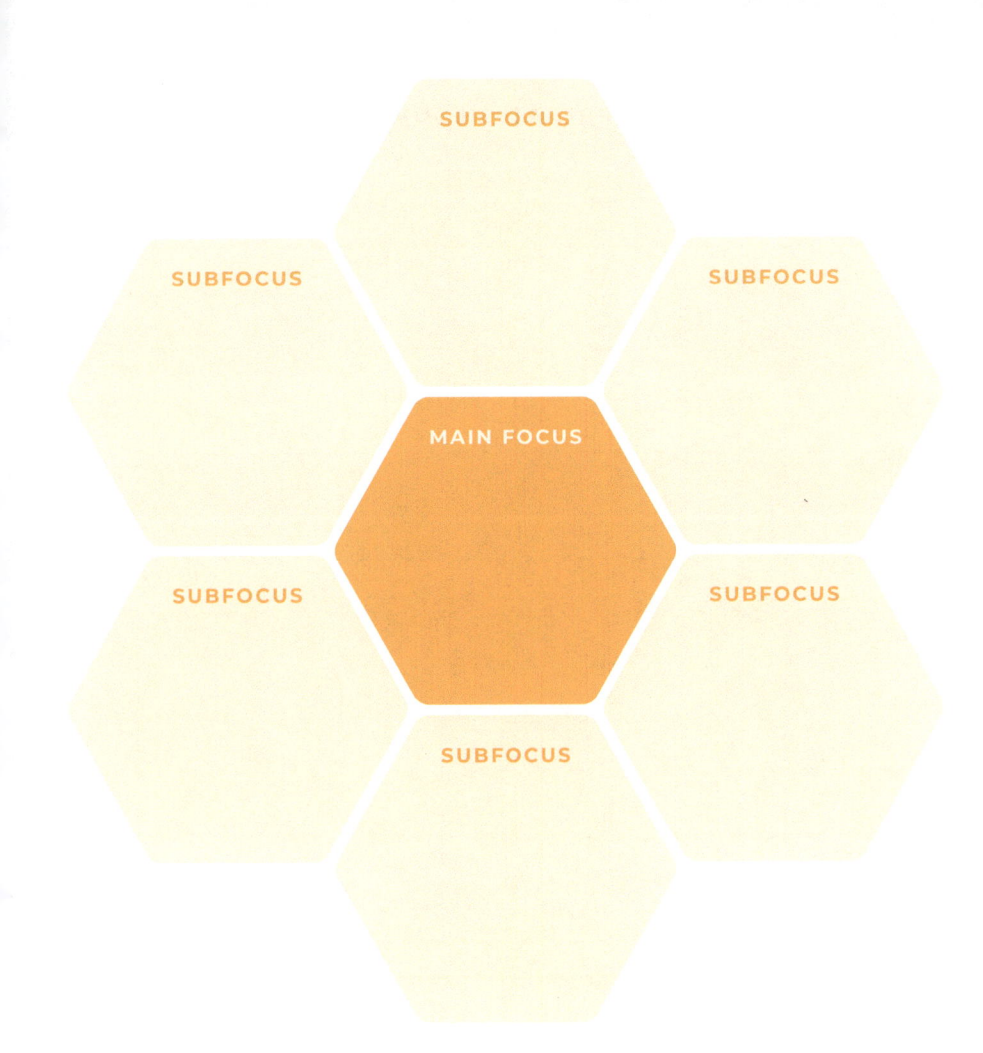

SUBFOCUS

SUBFOCUS

SUBFOCUS

SYMBOLIC	▶	INTERPRETATION	▶	
SYMBOLIC	▶	INTERPRETATION	▶	
SYMBOLIC	▶	INTERPRETATION	▶	
SYMBOLIC	▶	INTERPRETATION	▶	
SYMBOLIC	▶	INTERPRETATION	▶	
SYMBOLIC	▶	INTERPRETATION	▶	
SYMBOLIC	▶	INTERPRETATION	▶	

INTERPRETATION SUMMARY

APPLICATION

Dream Title

Dream Title

DAY OF THE WEEK
S M T W T F S

DATE
/ /

PRIMARY EMOTION
+ / −

DREAM CONTENT

One-third of our life is spent asleep. By the time we are sixty years old, we will have slept for about twenty years.

Dream Mapping

TYPE(S) OF DREAM *(Check all that apply)*

- Body Dream
- Soul Dream
- Demonic Dream
- God Dream

LENSES OF INTERPRETATION *(Check once completed)*

- Holy Spirit
- Emotion
- Dreamer's Personal / Cultural Experience
- Interpreter's Personal / Cultural Experience

MAIN FOCUS ▶	▶ LITERAL
SUBFOCUS ▶	▶ LITERAL
SUBFOCUS ▶	▶ LITERAL
SUBFOCUS ▶	▶ LITERAL
SUBFOCUS ▶	▶ LITERAL
SUBFOCUS ▶	▶ LITERAL
SUBFOCUS ▶	▶ LITERAL

SUBFOCUS

SUBFOCUS

SUBFOCUS

MAIN FOCUS

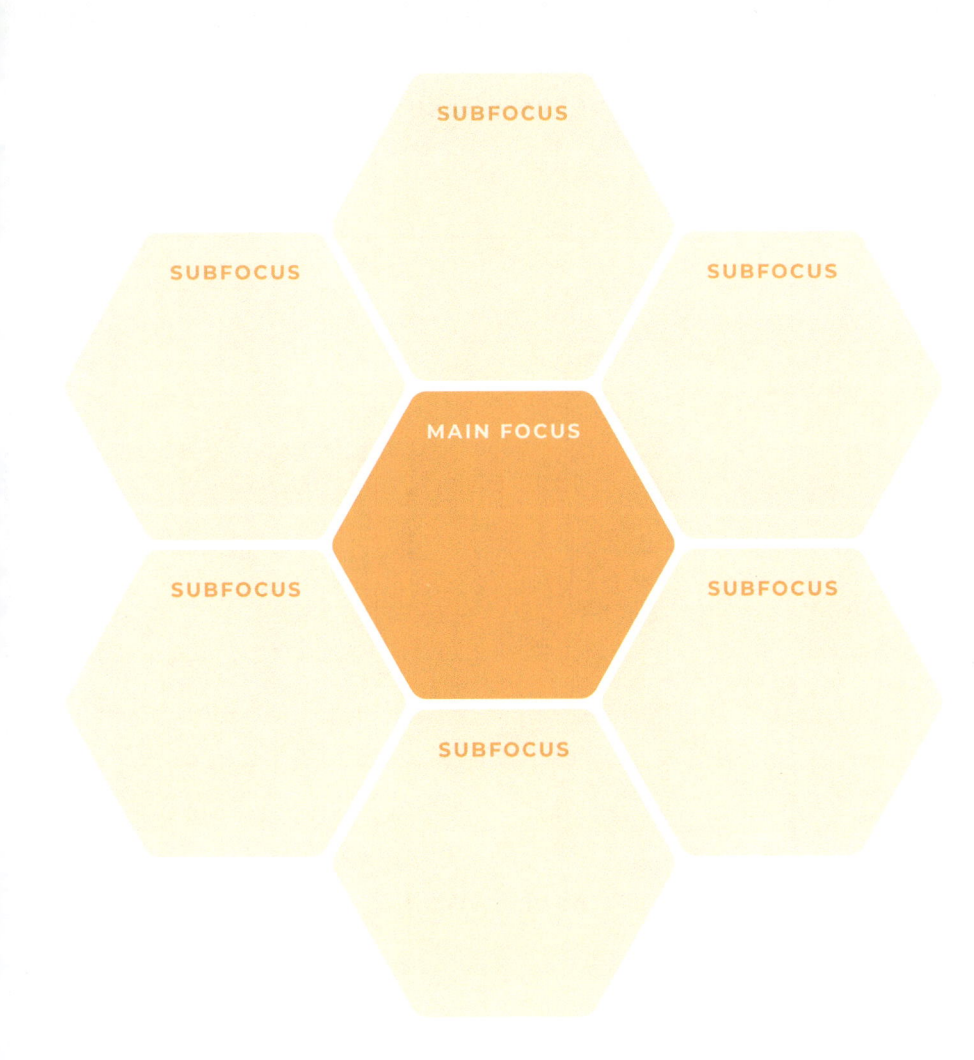

SUBFOCUS

SUBFOCUS

SUBFOCUS

SYMBOLIC	▶	INTERPRETATION	▶	
SYMBOLIC	▶	INTERPRETATION	▶	
SYMBOLIC	▶	INTERPRETATION	▶	
SYMBOLIC	▶	INTERPRETATION	▶	
SYMBOLIC	▶	INTERPRETATION	▶	
SYMBOLIC	▶	INTERPRETATION	▶	
SYMBOLIC	▶	INTERPRETATION	▶	

INTERPRETATION SUMMARY

APPLICATION

Dream Title

Dream Title

DAY OF THE WEEK
S M T W T F S

DATE
/ /

PRIMARY EMOTION
+ / −

DREAM CONTENT

_____
_____
_____
_____
_____
_____
_____
_____
_____
_____
_____
_____
_____
_____
_____
_____
_____
_____
_____
_____
_____
_____

*Dreams are a language of God's
intimacy with humanity.*

Dream Mapping

TYPE(S) OF DREAM *(Check all that apply)*

- Body Dream
- Soul Dream
- Demonic Dream
- God Dream

LENSES OF INTERPRETATION *(Check once completed)*

- Holy Spirit
- Emotion
- Dreamer's Personal / Cultural Experience
- Interpreter's Personal / Cultural Experience

MAIN FOCUS ▶	▶ LITERAL
SUBFOCUS ▶	▶ LITERAL
SUBFOCUS ▶	▶ LITERAL
SUBFOCUS ▶	▶ LITERAL
SUBFOCUS ▶	▶ LITERAL
SUBFOCUS ▶	▶ LITERAL
SUBFOCUS ▶	▶ LITERAL

SUBFOCUS

SUBFOCUS

SUBFOCUS

MAIN FOCUS

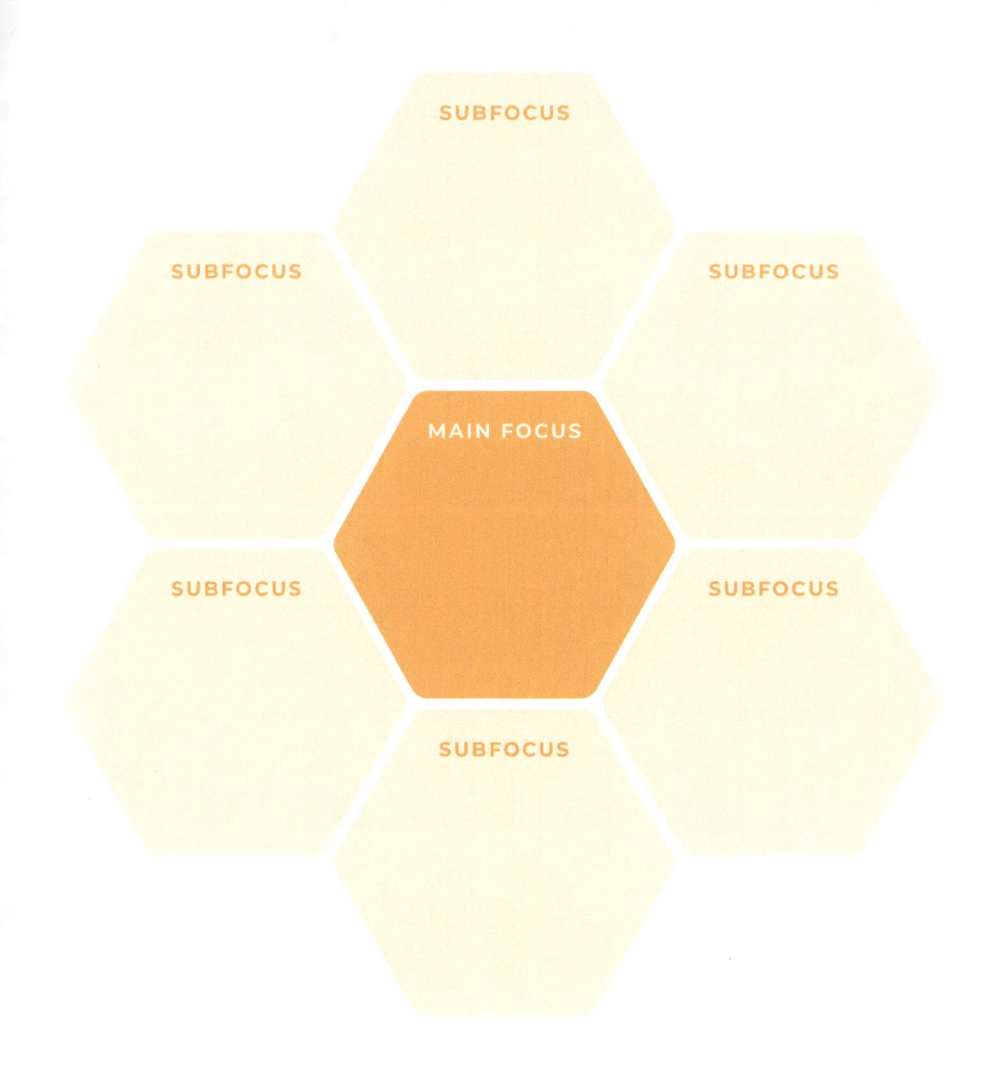

SUBFOCUS

SUBFOCUS

SUBFOCUS

SYMBOLIC	▶	INTERPRETATION	▶	
SYMBOLIC	▶	INTERPRETATION	▶	
SYMBOLIC	▶	INTERPRETATION	▶	
SYMBOLIC	▶	INTERPRETATION	▶	
SYMBOLIC	▶	INTERPRETATION	▶	
SYMBOLIC	▶	INTERPRETATION	▶	
SYMBOLIC	▶	INTERPRETATION	▶	

INTERPRETATION SUMMARY

APPLICATION

Dream Title

Dream Title

DAY OF THE WEEK

S　M　T　W　T　F　S

DATE

/　/

PRIMARY EMOTION

+　/　−

DREAM CONTENT

Depending on the context, repetitive dreams can be a good indicator that God is wanting to get your attention specifically to reveal or emphasize something.

Dream Mapping

TYPE(S) OF DREAM *(Check all that apply)*

- Body Dream
- Soul Dream
- Demonic Dream
- God Dream

LENSES OF INTERPRETATION *(Check once completed)*

- Holy Spirit
- Emotion
- Dreamer's Personal / Cultural Experience
- Interpreter's Personal / Cultural Experience

MAIN FOCUS	▶		▶	LITERAL
SUBFOCUS	▶		▶	LITERAL
SUBFOCUS	▶		▶	LITERAL
SUBFOCUS	▶		▶	LITERAL
SUBFOCUS	▶		▶	LITERAL
SUBFOCUS	▶		▶	LITERAL
SUBFOCUS	▶		▶	LITERAL

SUBFOCUS

SUBFOCUS

SUBFOCUS

MAIN FOCUS

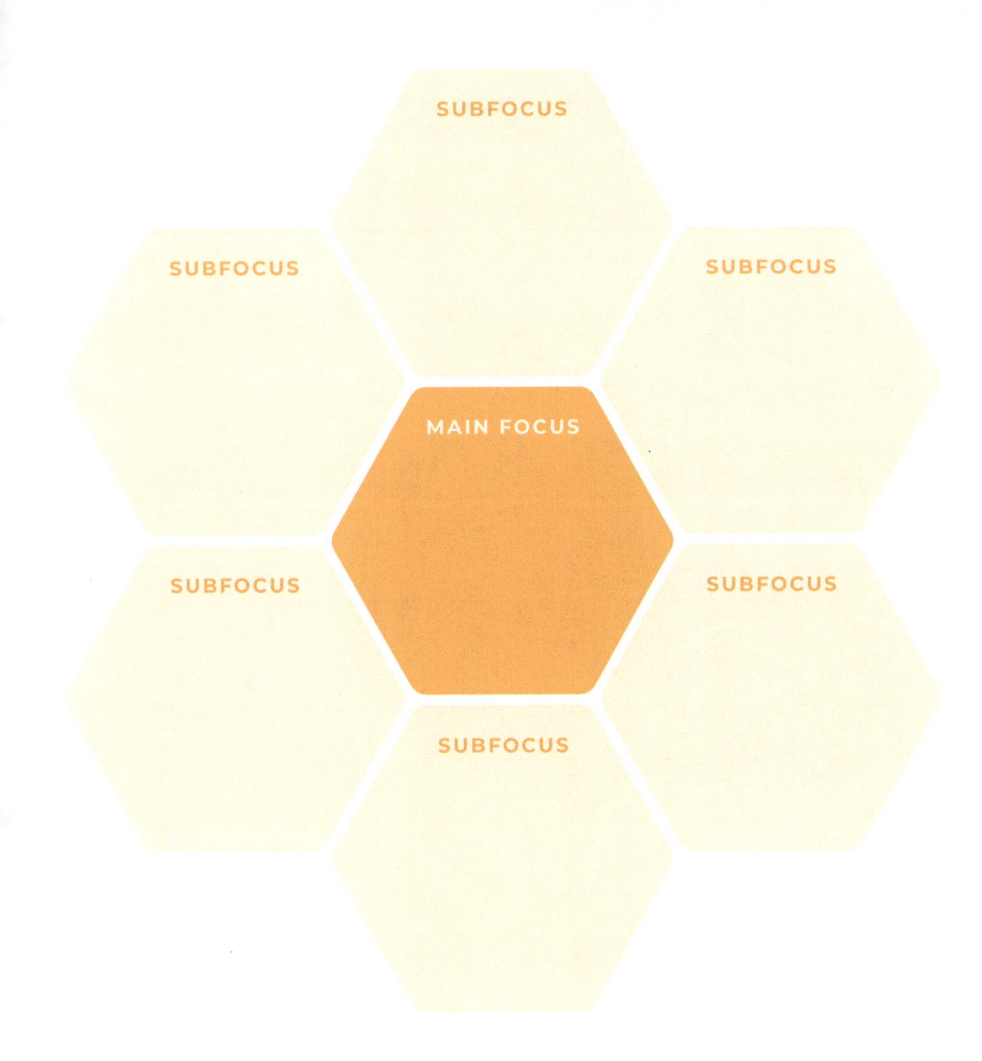

SUBFOCUS

SUBFOCUS

SUBFOCUS

SYMBOLIC	▶	INTERPRETATION	▶	
SYMBOLIC	▶	INTERPRETATION	▶	
SYMBOLIC	▶	INTERPRETATION	▶	
SYMBOLIC	▶	INTERPRETATION	▶	
SYMBOLIC	▶	INTERPRETATION	▶	
SYMBOLIC	▶	INTERPRETATION	▶	
SYMBOLIC	▶	INTERPRETATION	▶	

INTERPRETATION SUMMARY

APPLICATION

GOD IS
INVESTED
IN YOUR
SUCCESS

Dreaming with Purpose
DEVOTIONAL NO. 3

"In breeding season I once had a dream in which I looked up and saw that the male goats mating with the flock were streaked, speckled or spotted. The angel of God said to me in the dream, 'Jacob.' I answered, 'Here I am.' And he said, 'Look up and see that all the male goats mating with the flock are streaked, speckled or spotted, for I have seen all that Laban has been doing to you. I am the God of Bethel, where you anointed a pillar and where you made a vow to me. Now leave this land at once and go back to your native land.'"

// GENESIS 31:10–13 (NIV)

Does God care about your business, your success, your family, and your day-to-day life? Jacob, who had labored for his father-in-law, Laban, for fourteen years and had made him prosperous, had gained nothing for himself in the process. When Jacob called out to the Lord, God answered with divine strategy. He gave Jacob a dream, showing him how to cut stripes and spots in sticks and then put them in front of the sheep in the places where they drank and mated. In the natural world, this has no effect on the characteristics and appearance of sheep—but when God declares a thing, it becomes science. God is invested in your success. Wisdom and promotion may be just a dream away!

DEVOTIONAL NOTES

Dream Example

Coach "H" and the Prom Dreamer: Kira Armstrong

Dream Title

Coach "H" and the Prom

DAY OF THE WEEK
S M T (W) T F S

DATE
05 / 06 / 16

PRIMARY EMOTION
(+) / -

DREAM CONTENT

The week Kira had this dream, she had been asked to the junior/senior prom by a high school senior even though she was only a freshman.

Kira had talked to me and her mom a couple of times about what she should do. We prayed and left the decision up to her. One night that week she had a dream:

In the dream (later she told us), I was standing with all of the students from my high school in the quad area of the school as my track coach, whom the students affectionately called "Coach H" (short for her last name), was calling out assignments for the prom on a microphone. After calling out multiple assignments, she announced, "Kira Armstrong, your prom assignment is with Dalton."

It was a bit confusing in the dream because this was not the young man who had asked me to the prom in my waking life. Also, Dalton was a sophomore and I was a freshman; the prom was limited to juniors and seniors and their dates.

And God spoke to Israel in a vision at night and said, "Jacob! Jacob!" "Here I am," he replied. "I am God, the God of your father," he said. "Do not be afraid to go down to Egypt, for I will make you into a great nation there." (Genesis 46:2–3 NIV)

Dream Mapping

TYPE(S) OF DREAM *(Check all that apply)*

- ○ Body Dream
- ✗ Soul Dream
- ○ Demonic Dream
- ✗ God Dream

LENSES OF INTERPRETATION *(Check once completed)*

- ✗ Holy Spirit
- ✗ Emotion
- ✗ Dreamer's Personal / Cultural Experience
- ✗ Interpreter's Personal / Cultural Experience

MAIN FOCUS	▶	Kira	▶	**LITERAL**
SUBFOCUS	▶	prom	▶	**LITERAL**
SUBFOCUS	▶	Coach "H"	▶	LITERAL
SUBFOCUS	▶	friends	▶	**LITERAL**
SUBFOCUS	▶	Dalton	▶	LITERAL
SUBFOCUS	▶		▶	LITERAL
SUBFOCUS	▶		▶	LITERAL

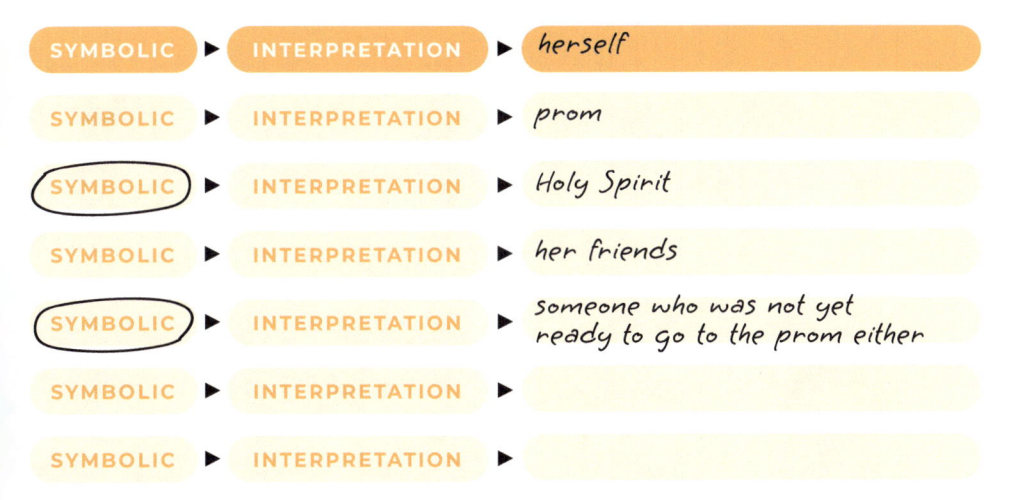

SUBFOCUS
SUBFOCUS
prom

SUBFOCUS
Coach "H"

MAIN FOCUS
Kira

SUBFOCUS
Dalton

SUBFOCUS
friends

SUBFOCUS

SYMBOLIC ▶	INTERPRETATION ▶	herself
SYMBOLIC ▶	INTERPRETATION ▶	prom
(SYMBOLIC) ▶	INTERPRETATION ▶	Holy Spirit
SYMBOLIC ▶	INTERPRETATION ▶	her friends
(SYMBOLIC) ▶	INTERPRETATION ▶	someone who was not yet ready to go to the prom either
SYMBOLIC ▶	INTERPRETATION ▶	
SYMBOLIC ▶	INTERPRETATION ▶	

INTERPRETATION SUMMARY

Going to the prom was important to Kira, and she wanted guidance in making what she saw as a hard decision. Dalton was not the young man who in her waking life had asked her to go to the prom; he was a sophomore at the time of the dream, which made him unable to invite anyone to the prom that year. Holy Spirit (in the form of Coach "H") was guiding Kira with the affirmation and courage to tell the young man who had invited her to the prom, "Not this year." This dream gave her the peace she needed to make that decision.

APPLICATION

Kira said, "Not this year, I don't feel ready to go to the prom," and she decided to hold off on going.

Dream Title

Dream Title

DAY OF THE WEEK

S M T W T F S

DATE

/ /

PRIMARY EMOTION

+ / −

DREAM CONTENT

Dreams and visions are very similar. The difference is that one is presented while we are awake and the other while we are asleep.

Dream Mapping

TYPE(S) OF DREAM *(Check all that apply)*

- Body Dream
- Soul Dream
- Demonic Dream
- God Dream

LENSES OF INTERPRETATION *(Check once completed)*

- Holy Spirit
- Emotion
- Dreamer's Personal / Cultural Experience
- Interpreter's Personal / Cultural Experience

MAIN FOCUS	▶		▶	LITERAL
SUBFOCUS	▶		▶	LITERAL
SUBFOCUS	▶		▶	LITERAL
SUBFOCUS	▶		▶	LITERAL
SUBFOCUS	▶		▶	LITERAL
SUBFOCUS	▶		▶	LITERAL
SUBFOCUS	▶		▶	LITERAL

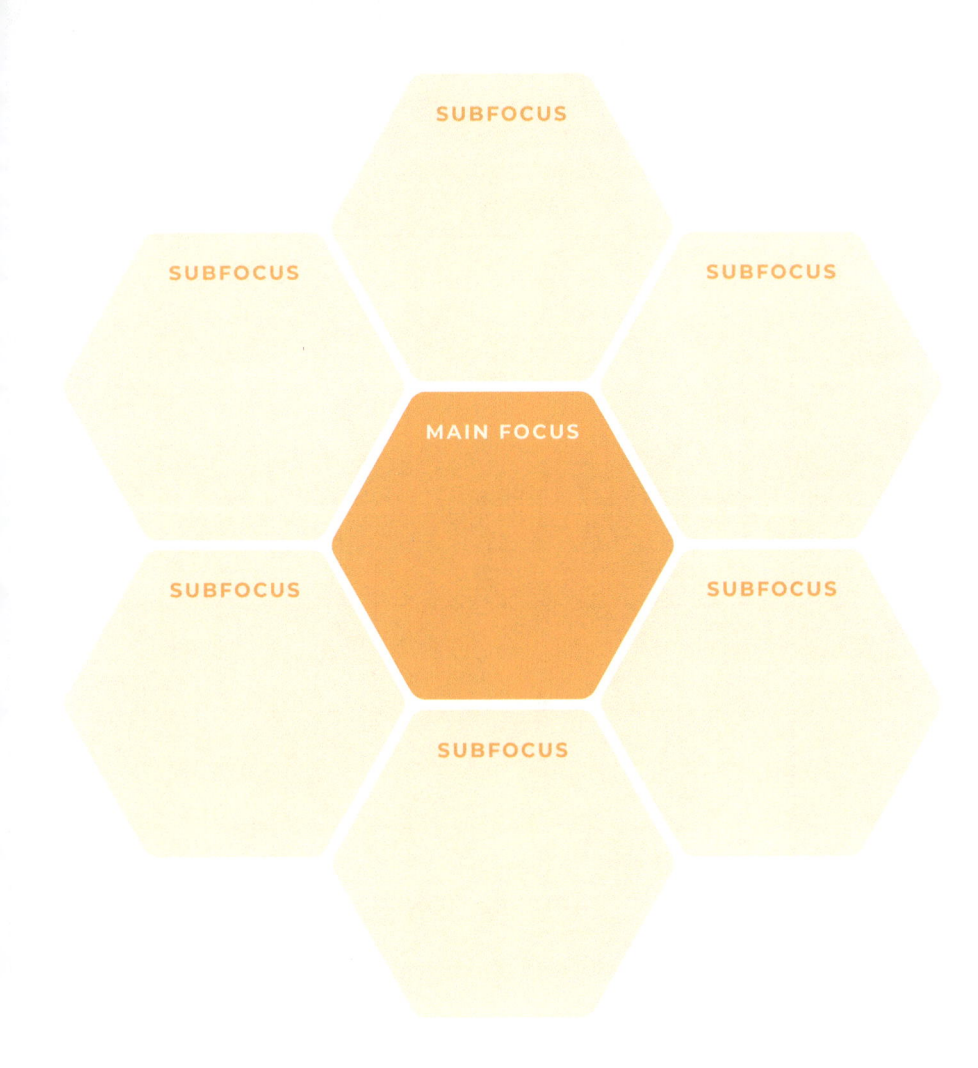

SUBFOCUS		
SUBFOCUS		
MAIN FOCUS		
SUBFOCUS		
SUBFOCUS		
SUBFOCUS		
SUBFOCUS		

SYMBOLIC	▶	INTERPRETATION	▶	
SYMBOLIC	▶	INTERPRETATION	▶	
SYMBOLIC	▶	INTERPRETATION	▶	
SYMBOLIC	▶	INTERPRETATION	▶	
SYMBOLIC	▶	INTERPRETATION	▶	
SYMBOLIC	▶	INTERPRETATION	▶	
SYMBOLIC	▶	INTERPRETATION	▶	

INTERPRETATION SUMMARY

APPLICATION

Dream Title

Dream Title

DAY OF THE WEEK	DATE	PRIMARY EMOTION
S M T W T F S	/ /	+ / −

DREAM CONTENT

The king said to Daniel, "Surely your God is the God of gods and the Lord of kings and a revealer of mysteries, for you were able to reveal this mystery."
(Daniel 2:47 NIV)

Dream Mapping

TYPE(S) OF DREAM *(Check all that apply)*

- Body Dream
- Soul Dream
- Demonic Dream
- God Dream

LENSES OF INTERPRETATION *(Check once completed)*

- Holy Spirit
- Emotion
- Dreamer's Personal / Cultural Experience
- Interpreter's Personal / Cultural Experience

MAIN FOCUS	▶		▶	LITERAL
SUBFOCUS	▶		▶	LITERAL
SUBFOCUS	▶		▶	LITERAL
SUBFOCUS	▶		▶	LITERAL
SUBFOCUS	▶		▶	LITERAL
SUBFOCUS	▶		▶	LITERAL
SUBFOCUS	▶		▶	LITERAL

SUBFOCUS

SUBFOCUS

SUBFOCUS

SUBFOCUS

MAIN FOCUS

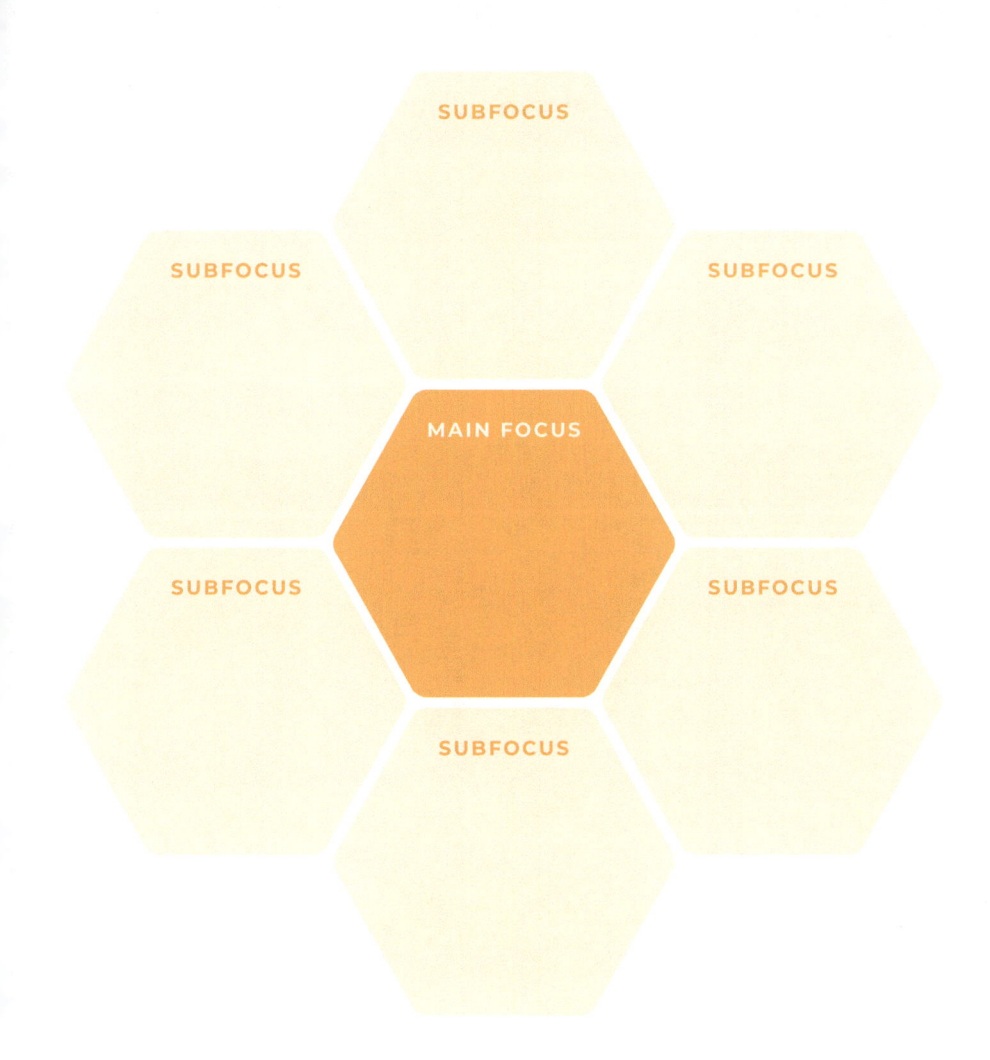

SUBFOCUS

SUBFOCUS

SUBFOCUS

SYMBOLIC	▶	INTERPRETATION	▶	
SYMBOLIC	▶	INTERPRETATION	▶	
SYMBOLIC	▶	INTERPRETATION	▶	
SYMBOLIC	▶	INTERPRETATION	▶	
SYMBOLIC	▶	INTERPRETATION	▶	
SYMBOLIC	▶	INTERPRETATION	▶	
SYMBOLIC	▶	INTERPRETATION	▶	

INTERPRETATION SUMMARY

APPLICATION

Dream Title

Dream Title

DAY OF THE WEEK	DATE	PRIMARY EMOTION
S M T W T F S	/ /	+ / −

DREAM CONTENT

_____
_____
_____
_____
_____
_____
_____
_____
_____
_____
_____
_____
_____
_____
_____
_____
_____
_____
_____
_____

The cycle of rest, renewal, and revelation was created by God.

Dream Mapping

TYPE(S) OF DREAM *(Check all that apply)*

- Body Dream
- Soul Dream
- Demonic Dream
- God Dream

LENSES OF INTERPRETATION *(Check once completed)*

- Holy Spirit
- Emotion
- Dreamer's Personal / Cultural Experience
- Interpreter's Personal / Cultural Experience

MAIN FOCUS	▶		▶	LITERAL
SUBFOCUS	▶		▶	LITERAL
SUBFOCUS	▶		▶	LITERAL
SUBFOCUS	▶		▶	LITERAL
SUBFOCUS	▶		▶	LITERAL
SUBFOCUS	▶		▶	LITERAL
SUBFOCUS	▶		▶	LITERAL

SUBFOCUS

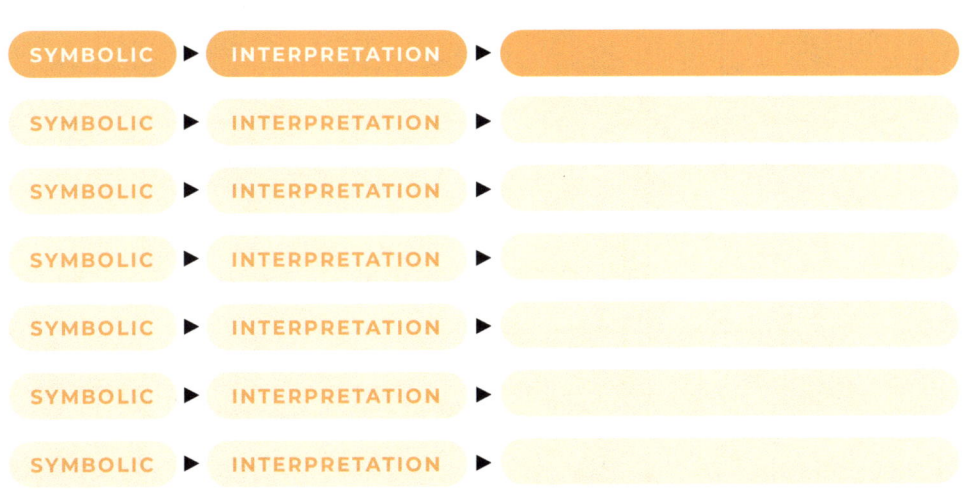

SUBFOCUS

SUBFOCUS

MAIN FOCUS

SUBFOCUS

SUBFOCUS

SUBFOCUS

SYMBOLIC	▶	INTERPRETATION	▶	
SYMBOLIC	▶	INTERPRETATION	▶	
SYMBOLIC	▶	INTERPRETATION	▶	
SYMBOLIC	▶	INTERPRETATION	▶	
SYMBOLIC	▶	INTERPRETATION	▶	
SYMBOLIC	▶	INTERPRETATION	▶	
SYMBOLIC	▶	INTERPRETATION	▶	

INTERPRETATION SUMMARY

APPLICATION

Dream Title

Dream Title

DAY OF THE WEEK
S M T W T F S

DATE
/ /

PRIMARY EMOTION
+ / −

DREAM CONTENT

*If you are actively participating in your own dream,
then most likely the dream is about you.*

Dream Mapping

TYPE(S) OF DREAM *(Check all that apply)*

- Body Dream
- Soul Dream
- Demonic Dream
- God Dream

LENSES OF INTERPRETATION *(Check once completed)*

- Holy Spirit
- Emotion
- Dreamer's Personal / Cultural Experience
- Interpreter's Personal / Cultural Experience

MAIN FOCUS ▶	▶ LITERAL
SUBFOCUS ▶	▶ LITERAL
SUBFOCUS ▶	▶ LITERAL
SUBFOCUS ▶	▶ LITERAL
SUBFOCUS ▶	▶ LITERAL
SUBFOCUS ▶	▶ LITERAL
SUBFOCUS ▶	▶ LITERAL

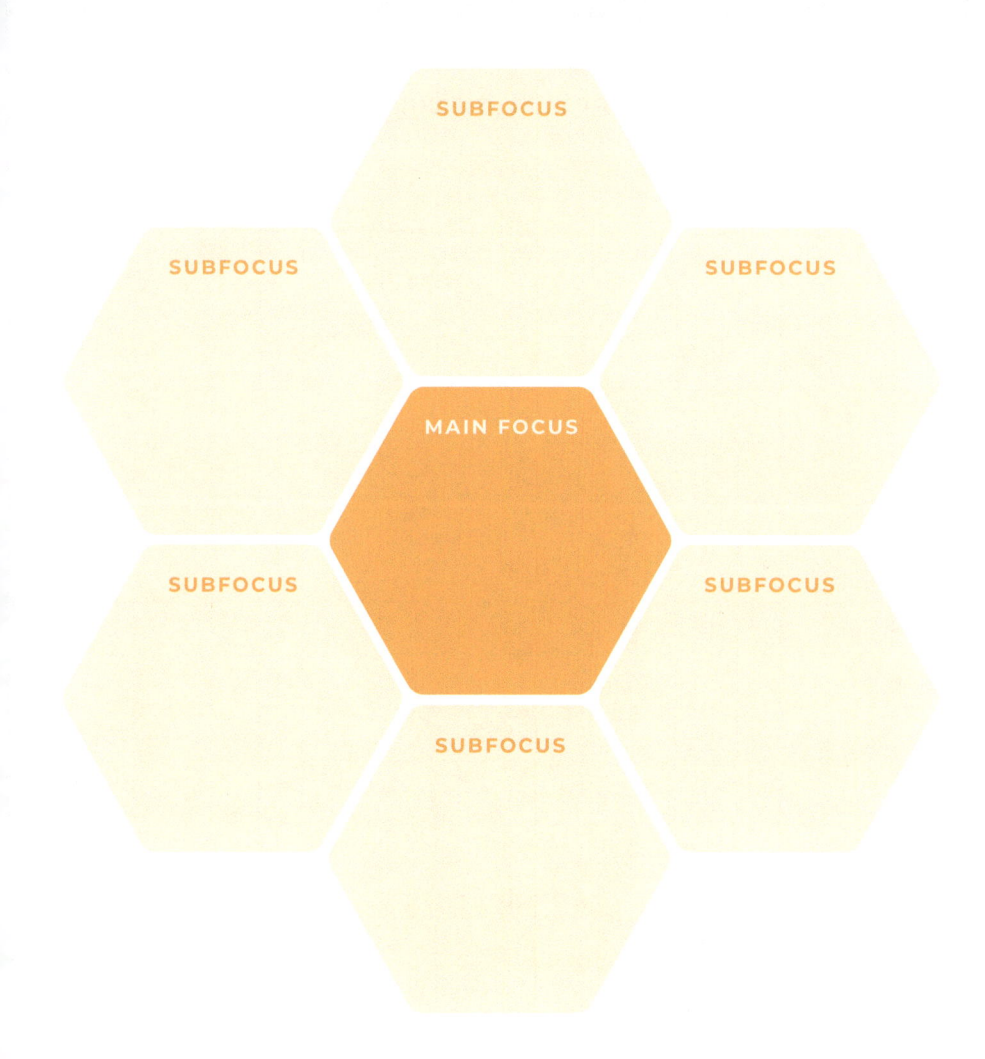

SUBFOCUS		
SUBFOCUS		SUBFOCUS
MAIN FOCUS		
SUBFOCUS		SUBFOCUS
SUBFOCUS		

SYMBOLIC	▶	INTERPRETATION	▶	
SYMBOLIC	▶	INTERPRETATION	▶	
SYMBOLIC	▶	INTERPRETATION	▶	
SYMBOLIC	▶	INTERPRETATION	▶	
SYMBOLIC	▶	INTERPRETATION	▶	
SYMBOLIC	▶	INTERPRETATION	▶	
SYMBOLIC	▶	INTERPRETATION	▶	

INTERPRETATION SUMMARY

APPLICATION

Dream Title

Dream Title

DAY OF THE WEEK
S M T W T F S

DATE
/ /

PRIMARY EMOTION
+ / −

DREAM CONTENT

_____
_____
_____
_____
_____
_____
_____
_____
_____
_____
_____
_____
_____
_____
_____
_____
_____
_____
_____
_____
_____
_____
_____
_____

Your body is wired to recognize the spiritual realm.

Dream Mapping

TYPE(S) OF DREAM *(Check all that apply)*

- ○ Body Dream
- ○ Soul Dream
- ○ Demonic Dream
- ○ God Dream

LENSES OF INTERPRETATION *(Check once completed)*

- ○ Holy Spirit
- ○ Emotion
- ○ Dreamer's Personal / Cultural Experience
- ○ Interpreter's Personal / Cultural Experience

MAIN FOCUS	▶		▶	LITERAL
SUBFOCUS	▶		▶	LITERAL
SUBFOCUS	▶		▶	LITERAL
SUBFOCUS	▶		▶	LITERAL
SUBFOCUS	▶		▶	LITERAL
SUBFOCUS	▶		▶	LITERAL
SUBFOCUS	▶		▶	LITERAL

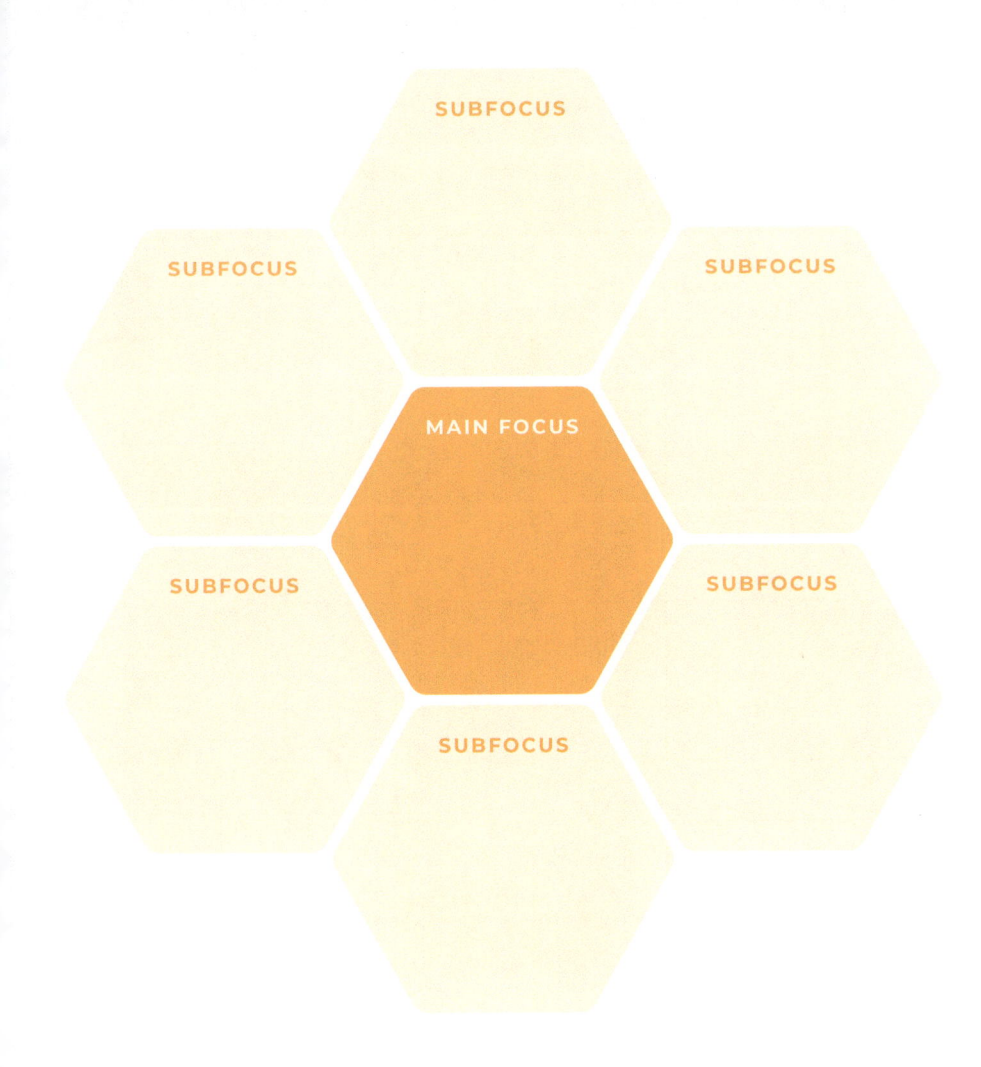

SUBFOCUS		SUBFOCUS
SUBFOCUS	MAIN FOCUS	SUBFOCUS
SUBFOCUS	SUBFOCUS	

SYMBOLIC ▶ **INTERPRETATION** ▶ _____

SYMBOLIC ▶ INTERPRETATION ▶ _____

SYMBOLIC ▶ INTERPRETATION ▶ _____

SYMBOLIC ▶ INTERPRETATION ▶ _____

SYMBOLIC ▶ INTERPRETATION ▶ _____

SYMBOLIC ▶ INTERPRETATION ▶ _____

SYMBOLIC ▶ INTERPRETATION ▶ _____

INTERPRETATION SUMMARY

APPLICATION

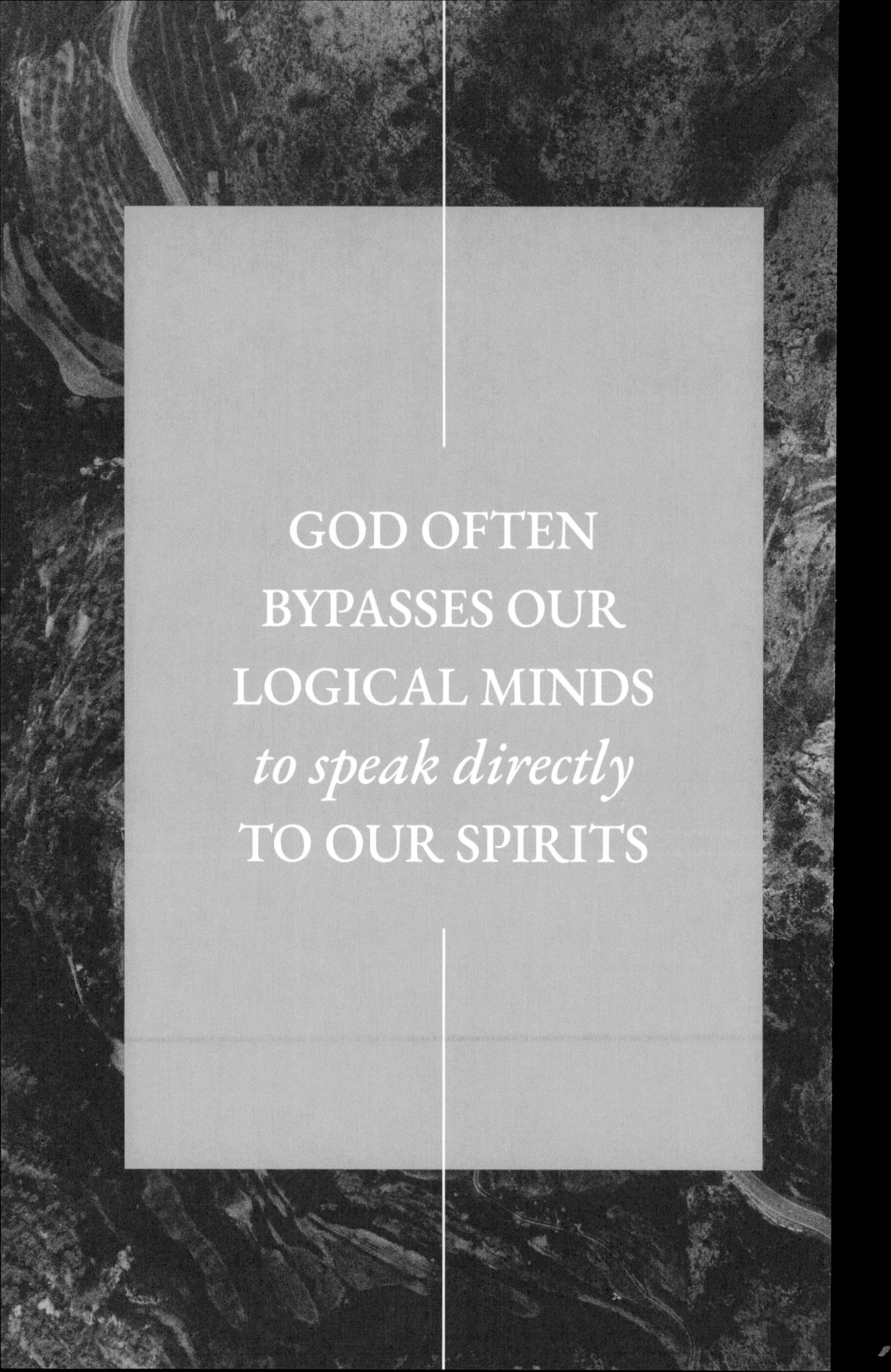

GOD OFTEN
BYPASSES OUR
LOGICAL MINDS
to speak directly
TO OUR SPIRITS

Unlocking Wisdom in Dreams

DEVOTIONAL NO. 4

In Gibeon the Lord appeared to Solomon in a dream at night; and God said, "Ask what you wish Me to give you." Then Solomon said, "You have shown great lovingkindness to Your servant David my father, according as he walked before You in truth and righteousness and uprightness of heart toward You; and You have reserved for him this great lovingkindness, that You have given him a son to sit on his throne, as it is this day. Now, O Lord my God, You have made Your servant king in place of my father David, yet I am but a little child; I do not know how to go out or come in. Your servant is in the midst of Your people which You have chosen, a great people who are too many to be numbered or counted. So give Your servant an understanding heart to judge Your people to discern between good and evil. For who is able to judge this great people of Yours?" It was pleasing in the sight of the Lord that Solomon had asked this thing. God said to him, "Because you have asked this thing and have not asked for yourself long life, nor have asked riches for yourself, nor have you asked for the life of your enemies, but have asked for yourself discernment to understand justice, behold, I have done according to your words. Behold, I have given you a wise and discerning heart, so that there has been no one like you before you, nor shall one like you arise after you. I have also given you what you have not asked, both riches and honor, so that there will not be any among the kings like you all your days. If you walk in My ways, keeping My statutes and commandments, as your father David walked, then I will prolong your days." Then Solomon awoke, and behold, it was a dream. And he came to Jerusalem and stood before the ark of the covenant of the Lord, and offered burnt offerings and made peace offerings, and made a feast for all his servants. // 1 KINGS 3:5–15 (NASB)

Solomon's wisdom was imparted to him through an encounter with God in a dream. Why did God wait until Solomon was asleep to ask him what he wanted? I think it's because God wanted to get around Solomon's rational mind and speak directly to his spirit. Like most people, I think that if God asks me what I want, one of the first things that would come to my mind is provision. "If I just had this amount, God, I could do so much for You! I would be so successful!" Or maybe I would think, "If You could just solve all my problems with other people, and I had no enemies, that would be perfect." God will do some things in dreams that He will not do in our waking hours in order to bypass our logical minds and speak directly to our spirits.

DEVOTIONAL NOTES

Dream Title

Dream Title

DAY OF THE WEEK	DATE	PRIMARY EMOTION
S M T W T F S	/ /	+ / −

DREAM CONTENT

*When we have negative dreams, we want to first ask,
"God, what's Your redemptive purpose here?"*

Dream Mapping

TYPE(S) OF DREAM *(Check all that apply)*

- Body Dream
- Soul Dream
- Demonic Dream
- God Dream

LENSES OF INTERPRETATION *(Check once completed)*

- Holy Spirit
- Emotion
- Dreamer's Personal / Cultural Experience
- Interpreter's Personal / Cultural Experience

MAIN FOCUS ▶	▶ LITERAL
SUBFOCUS ▶	▶ LITERAL
SUBFOCUS ▶	▶ LITERAL
SUBFOCUS ▶	▶ LITERAL
SUBFOCUS ▶	▶ LITERAL
SUBFOCUS ▶	▶ LITERAL
SUBFOCUS ▶	▶ LITERAL

SUBFOCUS

SUBFOCUS

SUBFOCUS

MAIN FOCUS

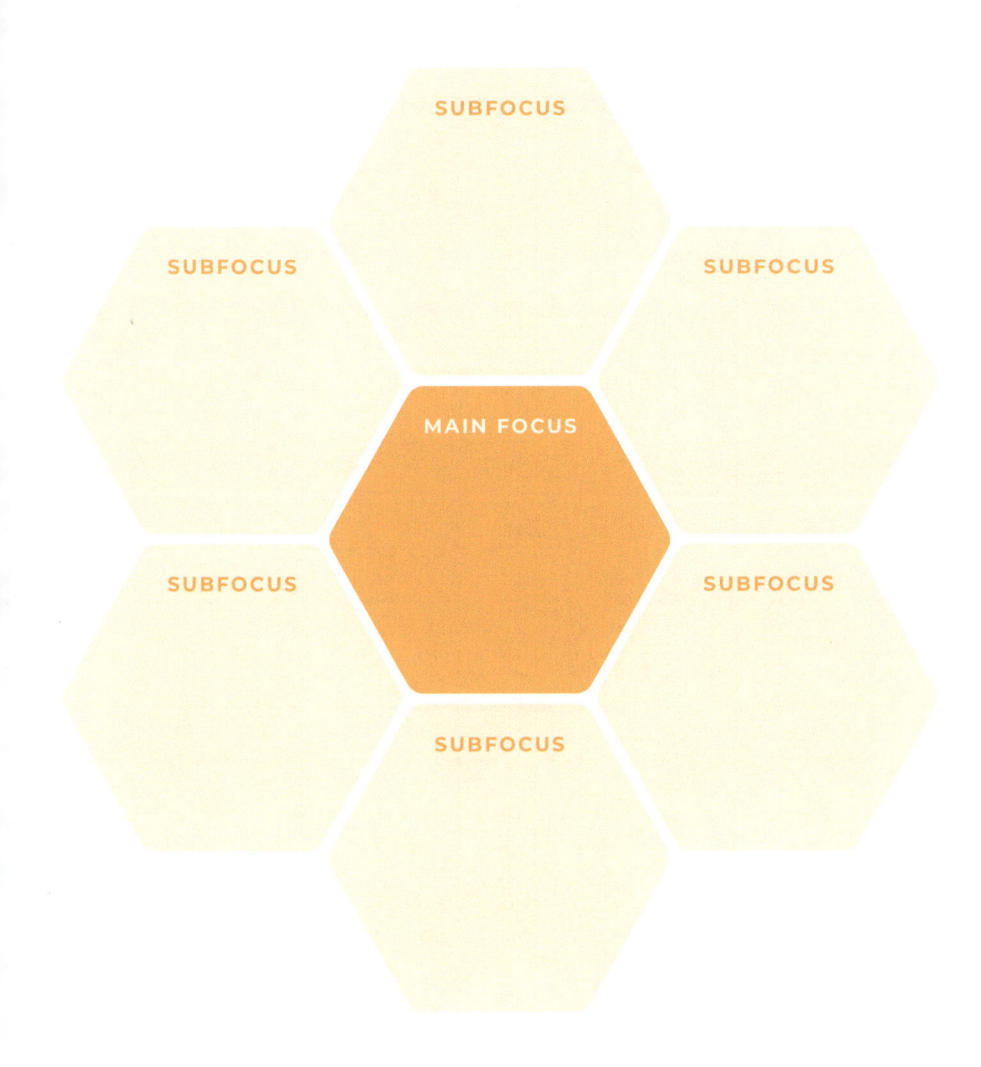

SUBFOCUS

SUBFOCUS

SUBFOCUS

SYMBOLIC	▶	INTERPRETATION	▶	
SYMBOLIC	▶	INTERPRETATION	▶	
SYMBOLIC	▶	INTERPRETATION	▶	
SYMBOLIC	▶	INTERPRETATION	▶	
SYMBOLIC	▶	INTERPRETATION	▶	
SYMBOLIC	▶	INTERPRETATION	▶	
SYMBOLIC	▶	INTERPRETATION	▶	

INTERPRETATION SUMMARY

APPLICATION

Dream Title

Dream Title

DAY OF THE WEEK

S M T W T F S

DATE

/   /

PRIMARY EMOTION

+   /   −

DREAM CONTENT

Day to day pours forth speech, And night to night reveals knowledge.
(Psalm 19:2 NASB)

Dream Mapping

TYPE(S) OF DREAM *(Check all that apply)*

- ○ Body Dream
- ○ Soul Dream
- ○ Demonic Dream
- ○ God Dream

LENSES OF INTERPRETATION *(Check once completed)*

- ○ Holy Spirit
- ○ Emotion
- ○ Dreamer's Personal / Cultural Experience
- ○ Interpreter's Personal / Cultural Experience

MAIN FOCUS	▶		▶	LITERAL
SUBFOCUS	▶		▶	LITERAL
SUBFOCUS	▶		▶	LITERAL
SUBFOCUS	▶		▶	LITERAL
SUBFOCUS	▶		▶	LITERAL
SUBFOCUS	▶		▶	LITERAL
SUBFOCUS	▶		▶	LITERAL

SUBFOCUS

SUBFOCUS

SUBFOCUS

MAIN FOCUS

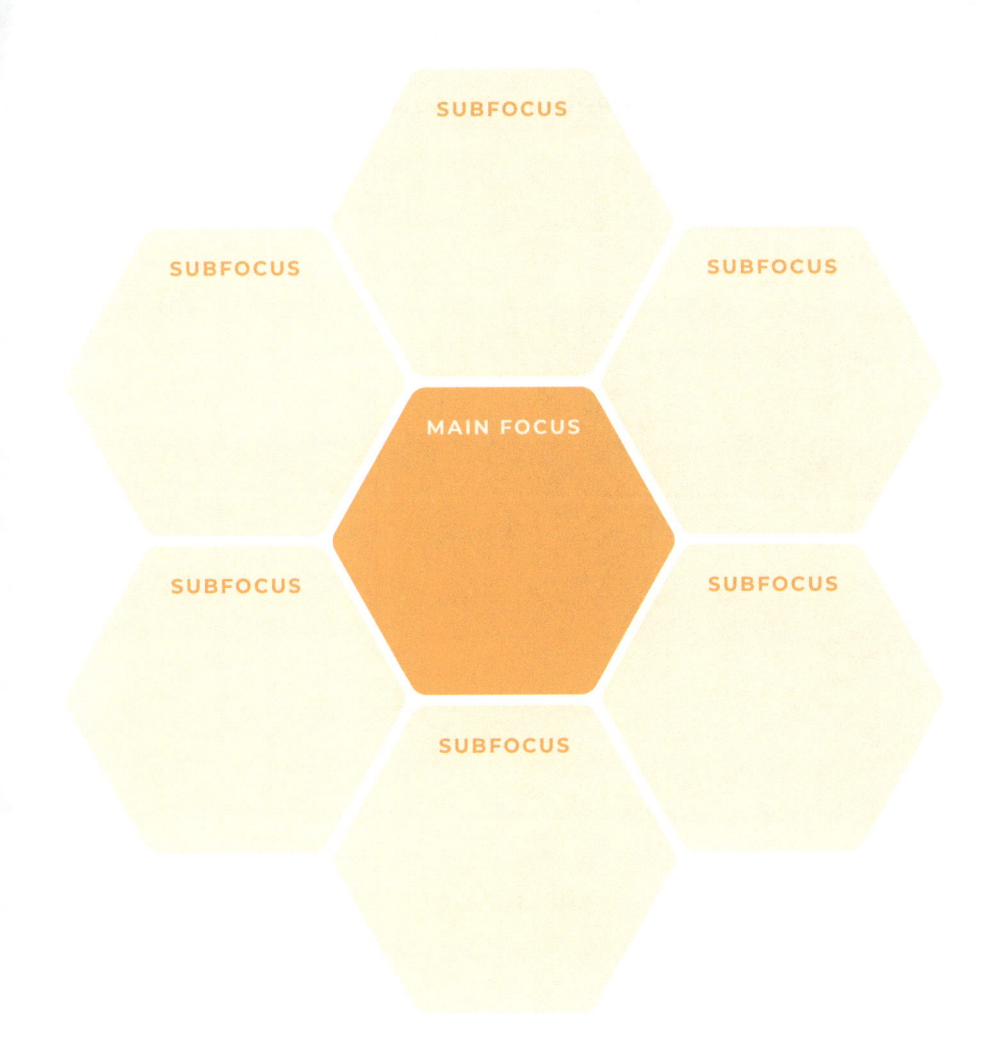

SUBFOCUS

SUBFOCUS

SUBFOCUS

SYMBOLIC	▶	INTERPRETATION	▶	
SYMBOLIC	▶	INTERPRETATION	▶	
SYMBOLIC	▶	INTERPRETATION	▶	
SYMBOLIC	▶	INTERPRETATION	▶	
SYMBOLIC	▶	INTERPRETATION	▶	
SYMBOLIC	▶	INTERPRETATION	▶	
SYMBOLIC	▶	INTERPRETATION	▶	

INTERPRETATION SUMMARY

APPLICATION

Dream Title

Dream Title

DAY OF THE WEEK	DATE	PRIMARY EMOTION
S M T W T F S	/ /	+ / −

DREAM CONTENT

*God has designed us to live from rest,
rather than for rest.*

Dream Mapping

TYPE(S) OF DREAM *(Check all that apply)*

- ○ Body Dream
- ○ Soul Dream
- ○ Demonic Dream
- ○ God Dream

LENSES OF INTERPRETATION *(Check once completed)*

- ○ Holy Spirit
- ○ Emotion
- ○ Dreamer's Personal / Cultural Experience
- ○ Interpreter's Personal / Cultural Experience

MAIN FOCUS	▶		▶	LITERAL
SUBFOCUS	▶		▶	LITERAL
SUBFOCUS	▶		▶	LITERAL
SUBFOCUS	▶		▶	LITERAL
SUBFOCUS	▶		▶	LITERAL
SUBFOCUS	▶		▶	LITERAL
SUBFOCUS	▶		▶	LITERAL

SUBFOCUS

SUBFOCUS

SUBFOCUS

MAIN FOCUS

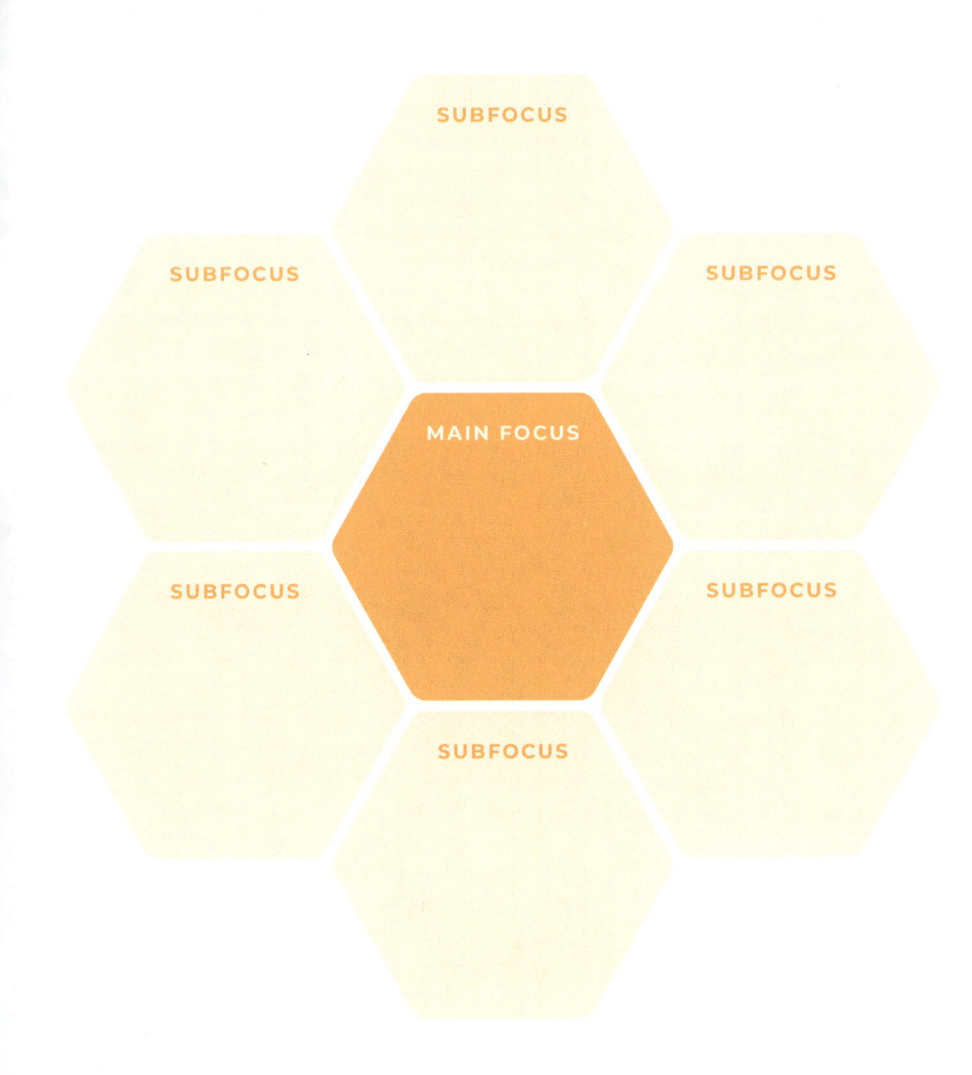

SUBFOCUS

SUBFOCUS

SUBFOCUS

SYMBOLIC	▶	INTERPRETATION	▶	
SYMBOLIC	▶	INTERPRETATION	▶	
SYMBOLIC	▶	INTERPRETATION	▶	
SYMBOLIC	▶	INTERPRETATION	▶	
SYMBOLIC	▶	INTERPRETATION	▶	
SYMBOLIC	▶	INTERPRETATION	▶	
SYMBOLIC	▶	INTERPRETATION	▶	

INTERPRETATION SUMMARY

APPLICATION

Dream Title

Dream Title

DAY OF THE WEEK
S M T W T F S

DATE
/ /

PRIMARY EMOTION
+ / −

DREAM CONTENT

The positive or negative emotion we have in our dream becomes one of the primary lenses through which we look to interpret its details.

Dream Mapping

TYPE(S) OF DREAM *(Check all that apply)*

- Body Dream
- Soul Dream
- Demonic Dream
- God Dream

LENSES OF INTERPRETATION *(Check once completed)*

- Holy Spirit
- Emotion
- Dreamer's Personal / Cultural Experience
- Interpreter's Personal / Cultural Experience

MAIN FOCUS	▶		▶	LITERAL
SUBFOCUS	▶		▶	LITERAL
SUBFOCUS	▶		▶	LITERAL
SUBFOCUS	▶		▶	LITERAL
SUBFOCUS	▶		▶	LITERAL
SUBFOCUS	▶		▶	LITERAL
SUBFOCUS	▶		▶	LITERAL

SUBFOCUS		
SUBFOCUS	SUBFOCUS	
	MAIN FOCUS	
SUBFOCUS	SUBFOCUS	
	SUBFOCUS	

- **SYMBOLIC** ▸ **INTERPRETATION** ▸ _____
- SYMBOLIC ▸ INTERPRETATION ▸ _____
- SYMBOLIC ▸ INTERPRETATION ▸ _____
- SYMBOLIC ▸ INTERPRETATION ▸ _____
- SYMBOLIC ▸ INTERPRETATION ▸ _____
- SYMBOLIC ▸ INTERPRETATION ▸ _____
- SYMBOLIC ▸ INTERPRETATION ▸ _____

INTERPRETATION SUMMARY

APPLICATION

Dream Title

Dream Title

DAY OF THE WEEK	DATE	PRIMARY EMOTION
S M T W T F S	/ /	+ / −

DREAM CONTENT

In Hebrew culture, your day starts at night.

Dream Mapping

TYPE(S) OF DREAM *(Check all that apply)*

- Body Dream
- Soul Dream
- Demonic Dream
- God Dream

LENSES OF INTERPRETATION *(Check once completed)*

- Holy Spirit
- Emotion
- Dreamer's Personal / Cultural Experience
- Interpreter's Personal / Cultural Experience

MAIN FOCUS	▶		▶	LITERAL
SUBFOCUS	▶		▶	LITERAL
SUBFOCUS	▶		▶	LITERAL
SUBFOCUS	▶		▶	LITERAL
SUBFOCUS	▶		▶	LITERAL
SUBFOCUS	▶		▶	LITERAL
SUBFOCUS	▶		▶	LITERAL

SUBFOCUS

SUBFOCUS

SUBFOCUS

MAIN FOCUS

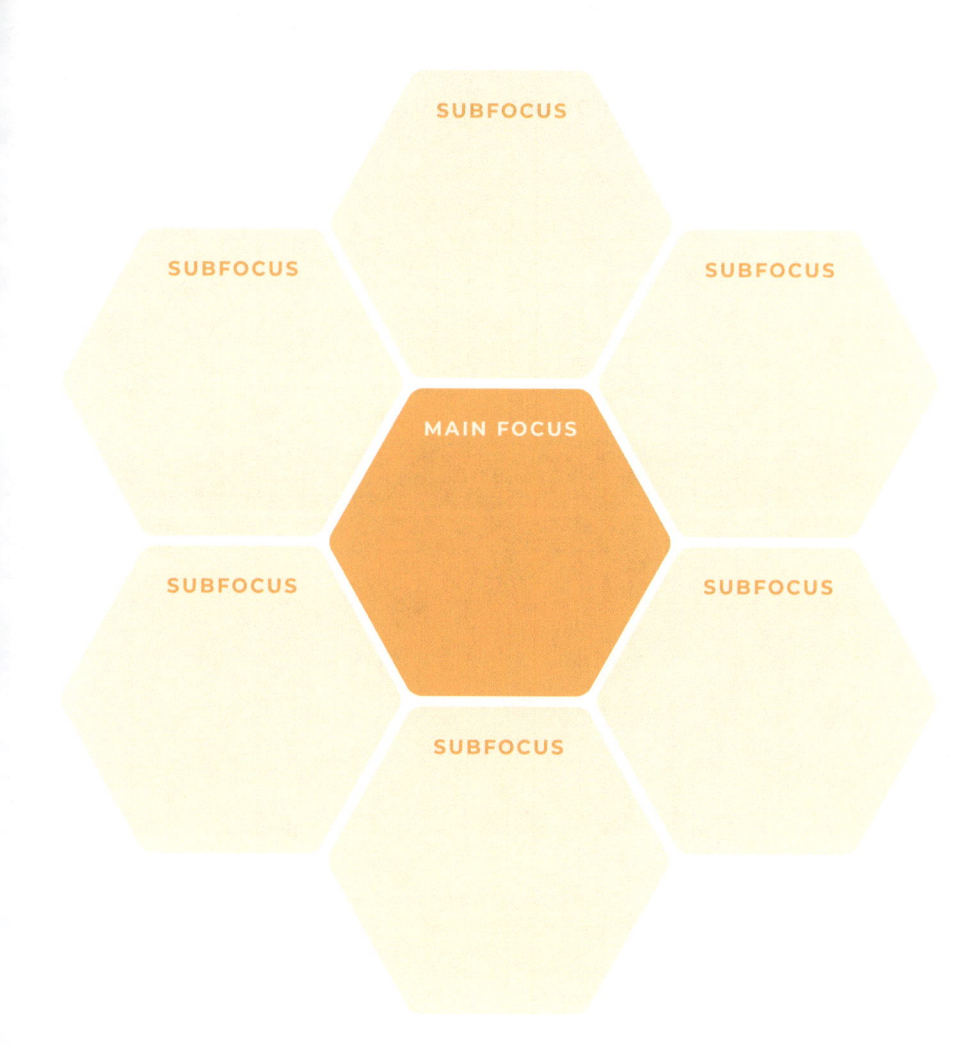

SUBFOCUS

SUBFOCUS

SUBFOCUS

SYMBOLIC	▶	INTERPRETATION	▶	
SYMBOLIC	▶	INTERPRETATION	▶	
SYMBOLIC	▶	INTERPRETATION	▶	
SYMBOLIC	▶	INTERPRETATION	▶	
SYMBOLIC	▶	INTERPRETATION	▶	
SYMBOLIC	▶	INTERPRETATION	▶	
SYMBOLIC	▶	INTERPRETATION	▶	

INTERPRETATION SUMMARY

APPLICATION

WITHOUT GOD
it is impossible
TO ACCURATELY
INTERPRET
OUR DREAMS

The Gift of Dream Interpretation

DEVOTIONAL NO. 5

"We both had dreams," they answered, "but there is no one to interpret them." Then Joseph said to them, "Do not interpretations belong to God? Tell me your dreams."
// GENESIS 40:8 (NIV)

Daniel replied, "No wise man, enchanter, magician or diviner can explain to the king the mystery he has asked about, but there is a God in heaven who reveals mysteries. He has shown King Nebuchadnezzar what will happen in days to come. Your dream and the visions that passed through your mind as you were lying in bed are these..."
// DANIEL 2:27–28 (NIV)

Joseph knew interpretation and wisdom come from God Himself. Without God, it is impossible to accurately interpret our dreams. Dreams and dream interpretation are a beautiful source of connection to God.

DEVOTIONAL NOTES

Dream Example

Thrift Store Shopping
Dreamer: Madison Armstrong

Dream Title

Thrift Store Shopping

DAY OF THE WEEK
S M (T) W T F S

DATE
05/12/17

PRIMARY EMOTION
(+) / −

DREAM CONTENT

In the dream, I was thrift-store shopping with my friend, Justice Cooper. When we walked into the store, there was an older lady behind the display counter. Justice and I walked to the counter, which was filled with rings for sale. As we looked at the different rings, the lady behind the counter pulled one out of the display, handed it to Justice, and said, "This is for you. You can keep it." I thought, "I want a ring, too," and although I didn't state it out loud, the lady behind the counter reached into the display and gave me a ring as well.

As we were admiring our rings, the bell that announced the entrance of another customer coming through the door rang. We looked at the door and saw it was a young blonde lady. The moment I saw her, I thought, "This lady has had a miscarriage." The lady also walked to the display case, where she was greeted by the woman behind the counter. As Justice and I watched, the woman behind the counter reached behind her to a blue maternity dress that was hanging on the wall for display. She then gave it to the lady who had had a miscarriage.

During the night the mystery was revealed to Daniel in a vision. Then Daniel praised the God of heaven. (Daniel 2:19 NIV)

The scene in the dream shifted instantly and I was now cradling a bundled baby in my arms. I knew in the dream that it belonged to the lady who had once had a miscarriage.

Dream Mapping

TYPE(S) OF DREAM *(Check all that apply)*

- ○ Body Dream
- ○ Soul Dream
- ○ Demonic Dream
- ✗ God Dream

LENSES OF INTERPRETATION *(Check once completed)*

- ✗ Holy Spirit
- ✗ Emotion
- ✗ Dreamer's Personal / Cultural Experience
- ✗ Interpreter's Personal / Cultural Experience

MAIN FOCUS	▸	Madison	▸	**(LITERAL)**
SUBFOCUS	▸	Justice Cooper	▸	LITERAL
SUBFOCUS	▸	lady behind the counter	▸	LITERAL
SUBFOCUS	▸	ring	▸	LITERAL
SUBFOCUS	▸	young blonde lady	▸	LITERAL
SUBFOCUS	▸	blue maternity dress	▸	LITERAL
SUBFOCUS	▸	baby	▸	LITERAL

SUBFOCUS: Justice Cooper

SUBFOCUS: baby

SUBFOCUS: lady behind the counter

MAIN FOCUS: Madison

SUBFOCUS: blue maternity dress

SUBFOCUS: ring

SUBFOCUS: young blonde lady

SYMBOLIC ▸	INTERPRETATION ▸	herself
SYMBOLIC ▸	INTERPRETATION ▸	the justice of God
SYMBOLIC ▸	INTERPRETATION ▸	Holy Spirit
SYMBOLIC ▸	INTERPRETATION ▸	promise of covenant
SYMBOLIC ▸	INTERPRETATION ▸	women who have miscarried
SYMBOLIC ▸	INTERPRETATION ▸	promise of pregnancy
SYMBOLIC ▸	INTERPRETATION ▸	fulfilled promise

INTERPRETATION SUMMARY

Madison is friends with "Justice." She carries justice for women who have experienced the injustice of miscarriage. She has been given the authority to establish justice through intercession. She partners with the gift of the Holy Spirit to see pregnancy come to full term and women get the fulfilled promise of children.

APPLICATION

Madison and I have now shared the testimony of the dream and prayed over women who have had miscarriages. At least a dozen of these women have now carried their children to full term!

Dream Title

Dream Title

DAY OF THE WEEK
S M T W T F S

DATE
/   /

PRIMARY EMOTION
+   /   −

DREAM CONTENT

When you lie down, you will not be afraid; when you lie down, your sleep will be sweet. (Proverbs 3:24 NIV)

Dream Mapping

TYPE(S) OF DREAM *(Check all that apply)*

- Body Dream
- Soul Dream
- Demonic Dream
- God Dream

LENSES OF INTERPRETATION *(Check once completed)*

- Holy Spirit
- Emotion
- Dreamer's Personal / Cultural Experience
- Interpreter's Personal / Cultural Experience

MAIN FOCUS ▶	▶ LITERAL
SUBFOCUS ▶	▶ LITERAL
SUBFOCUS ▶	▶ LITERAL
SUBFOCUS ▶	▶ LITERAL
SUBFOCUS ▶	▶ LITERAL
SUBFOCUS ▶	▶ LITERAL
SUBFOCUS ▶	▶ LITERAL

SUBFOCUS

SUBFOCUS

SUBFOCUS

MAIN FOCUS

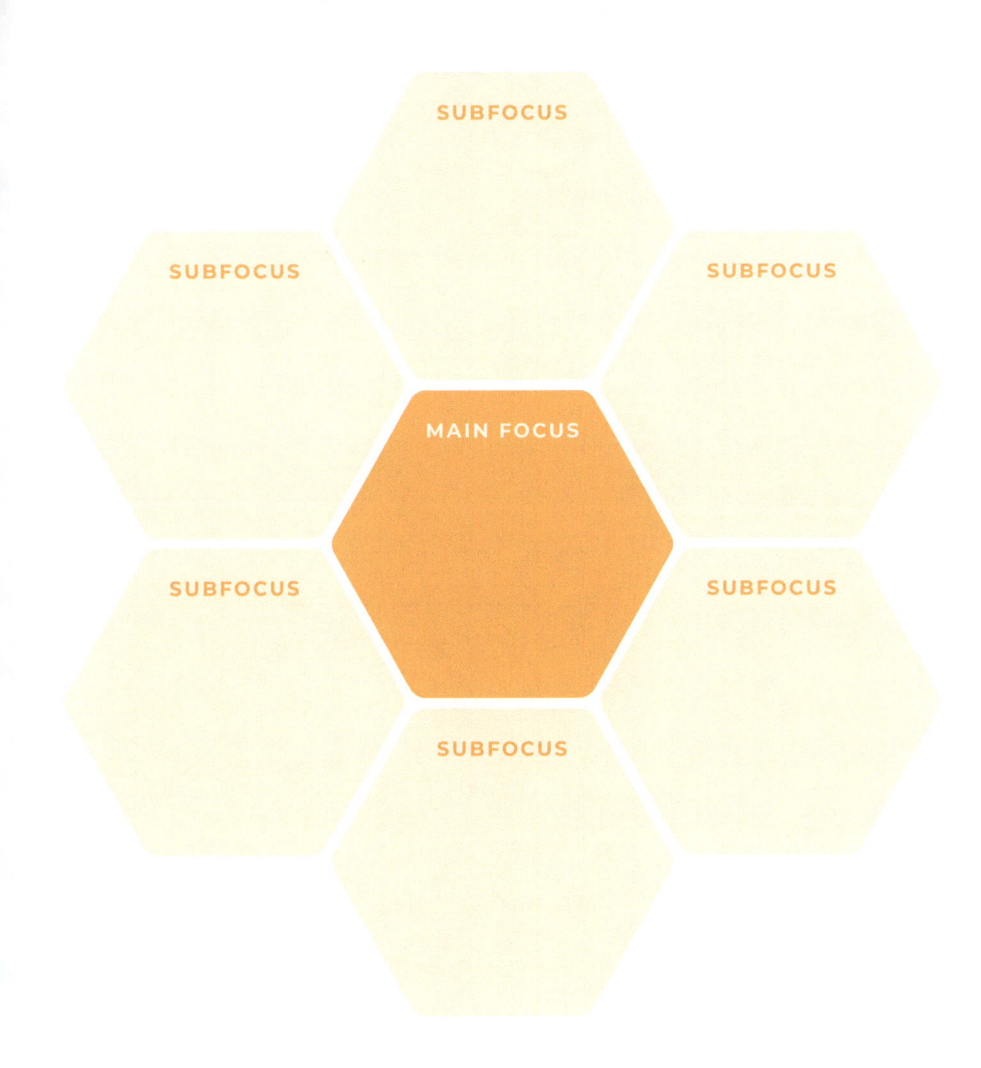

SUBFOCUS

SUBFOCUS

SUBFOCUS

SYMBOLIC	▶	INTERPRETATION	▶	
SYMBOLIC	▶	INTERPRETATION	▶	
SYMBOLIC	▶	INTERPRETATION	▶	
SYMBOLIC	▶	INTERPRETATION	▶	
SYMBOLIC	▶	INTERPRETATION	▶	
SYMBOLIC	▶	INTERPRETATION	▶	
SYMBOLIC	▶	INTERPRETATION	▶	

INTERPRETATION SUMMARY

APPLICATION

Dream Title

Dream Title

DAY OF THE WEEK	DATE	PRIMARY EMOTION
S M T W T F S	/ /	+ / −

DREAM CONTENT

God will sometimes try to get behind our rational mind and speak to us Spirit to spirit!

Dream Mapping

TYPE(S) OF DREAM *(Check all that apply)*

- ○ Body Dream
- ○ Soul Dream
- ○ Demonic Dream
- ○ God Dream

LENSES OF INTERPRETATION *(Check once completed)*

- ○ Holy Spirit
- ○ Emotion
- ○ Dreamer's Personal / Cultural Experience
- ○ Interpreter's Personal / Cultural Experience

MAIN FOCUS	▶		▶	LITERAL
SUBFOCUS	▶		▶	LITERAL
SUBFOCUS	▶		▶	LITERAL
SUBFOCUS	▶		▶	LITERAL
SUBFOCUS	▶		▶	LITERAL
SUBFOCUS	▶		▶	LITERAL
SUBFOCUS	▶		▶	LITERAL

SUBFOCUS

SUBFOCUS

SUBFOCUS

MAIN FOCUS

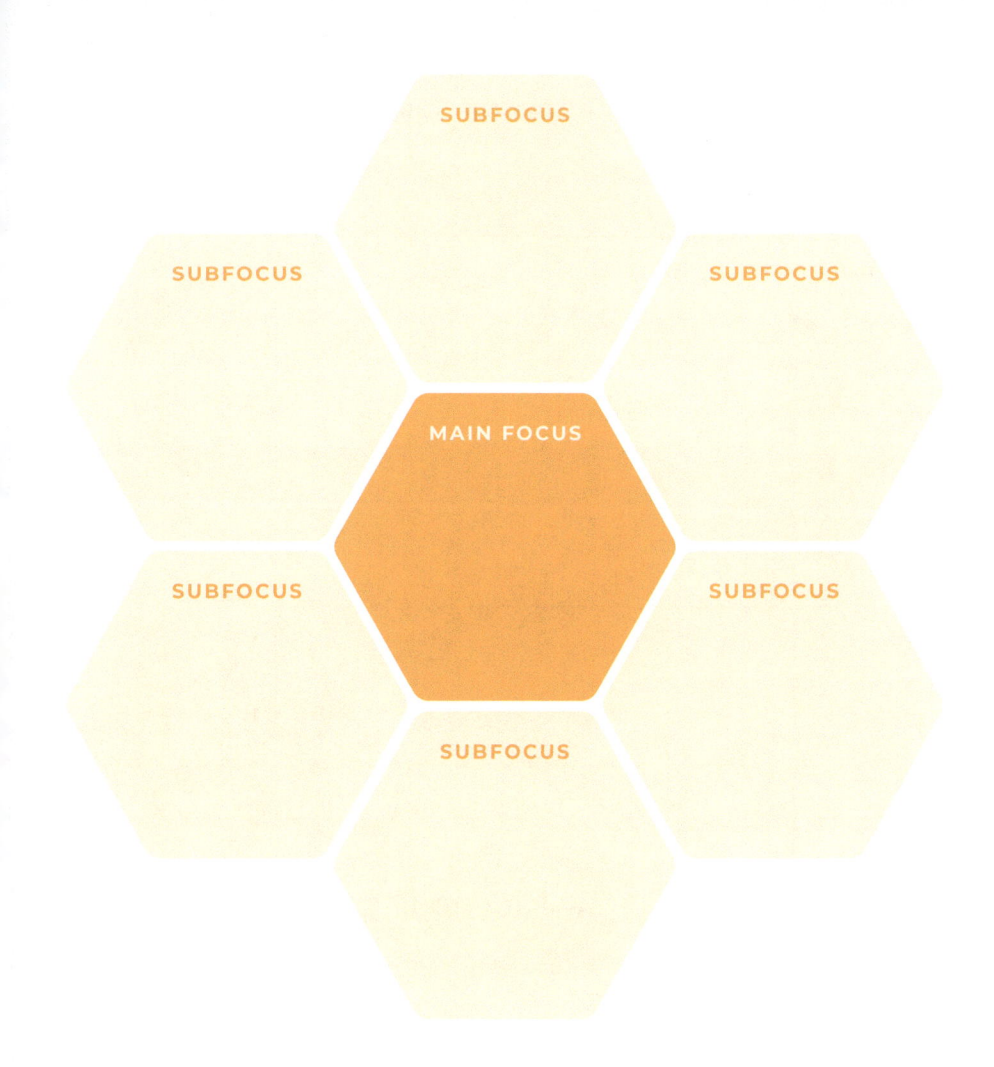

SUBFOCUS

SUBFOCUS

SUBFOCUS

SYMBOLIC ▶	INTERPRETATION ▶	
SYMBOLIC ▶	INTERPRETATION ▶	
SYMBOLIC ▶	INTERPRETATION ▶	
SYMBOLIC ▶	INTERPRETATION ▶	
SYMBOLIC ▶	INTERPRETATION ▶	
SYMBOLIC ▶	INTERPRETATION ▶	
SYMBOLIC ▶	INTERPRETATION ▶	

INTERPRETATION SUMMARY

APPLICATION

Dream Title

Dream Title

DAY OF THE WEEK	DATE	PRIMARY EMOTION
S M T W T F S	/ /	+ / −

DREAM CONTENT

*Whatever you focus on during the day
may show up at night.*

Dream Mapping

TYPE(S) OF DREAM *(Check all that apply)*

- Body Dream
- Soul Dream
- Demonic Dream
- God Dream

LENSES OF INTERPRETATION *(Check once completed)*

- Holy Spirit
- Emotion
- Dreamer's Personal / Cultural Experience
- Interpreter's Personal / Cultural Experience

MAIN FOCUS	▶		▶	LITERAL
SUBFOCUS	▶		▶	LITERAL
SUBFOCUS	▶		▶	LITERAL
SUBFOCUS	▶		▶	LITERAL
SUBFOCUS	▶		▶	LITERAL
SUBFOCUS	▶		▶	LITERAL
SUBFOCUS	▶		▶	LITERAL

SUBFOCUS

SUBFOCUS

SUBFOCUS

SUBFOCUS

MAIN FOCUS

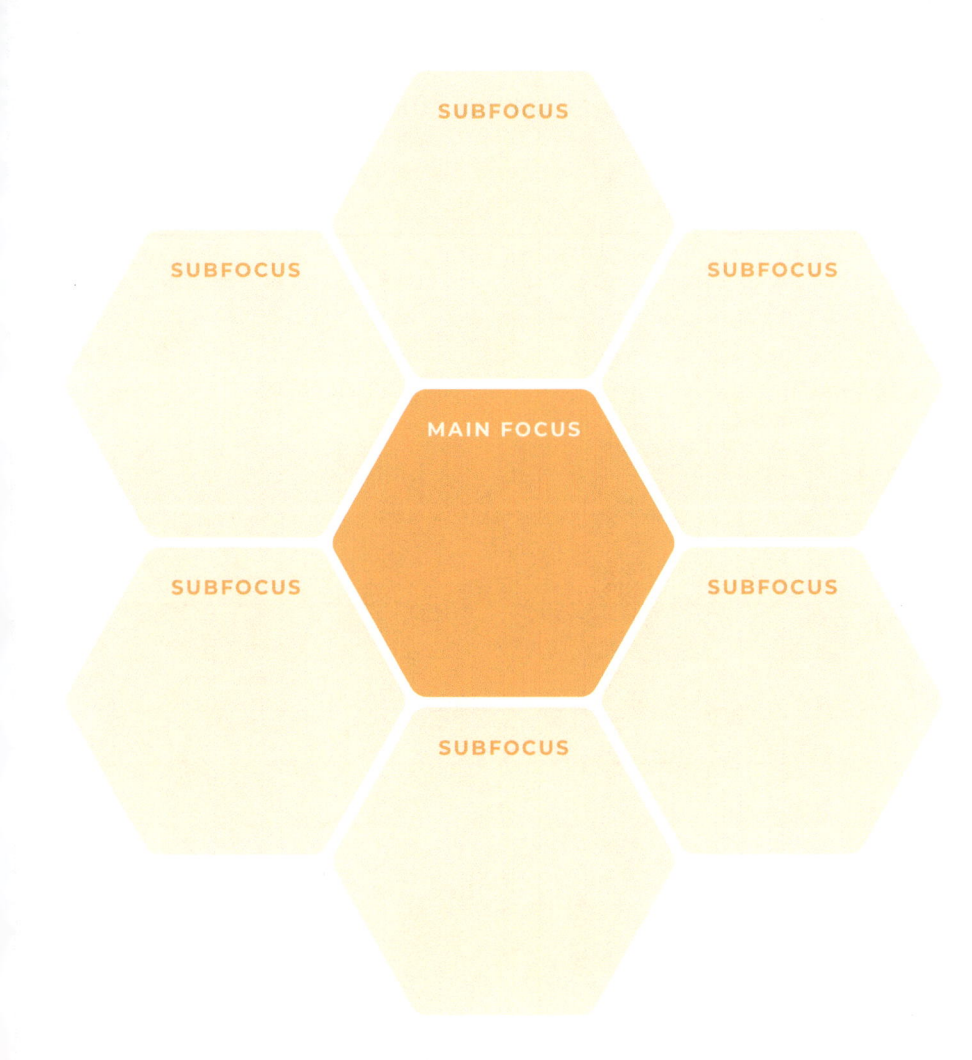

SUBFOCUS

SUBFOCUS

SUBFOCUS

SYMBOLIC	▶	INTERPRETATION	▶	
SYMBOLIC	▶	INTERPRETATION	▶	
SYMBOLIC	▶	INTERPRETATION	▶	
SYMBOLIC	▶	INTERPRETATION	▶	
SYMBOLIC	▶	INTERPRETATION	▶	
SYMBOLIC	▶	INTERPRETATION	▶	
SYMBOLIC	▶	INTERPRETATION	▶	

INTERPRETATION SUMMARY

APPLICATION

Dream Title

Dream Title

DAY OF THE WEEK
S M T W T F S

DATE
/ /

PRIMARY EMOTION
+ / −

DREAM CONTENT

It is sometimes the kindness of God to hide the meaning of a dream until He establishes a root system that can carry it to fruition.

Dream Mapping

TYPE(S) OF DREAM *(Check all that apply)*

- Body Dream
- Soul Dream
- Demonic Dream
- God Dream

LENSES OF INTERPRETATION *(Check once completed)*

- Holy Spirit
- Emotion
- Dreamer's Personal / Cultural Experience
- Interpreter's Personal / Cultural Experience

MAIN FOCUS ▶	▶ LITERAL
SUBFOCUS ▶	▶ LITERAL
SUBFOCUS ▶	▶ LITERAL
SUBFOCUS ▶	▶ LITERAL
SUBFOCUS ▶	▶ LITERAL
SUBFOCUS ▶	▶ LITERAL
SUBFOCUS ▶	▶ LITERAL

SUBFOCUS

SUBFOCUS

SUBFOCUS

MAIN FOCUS

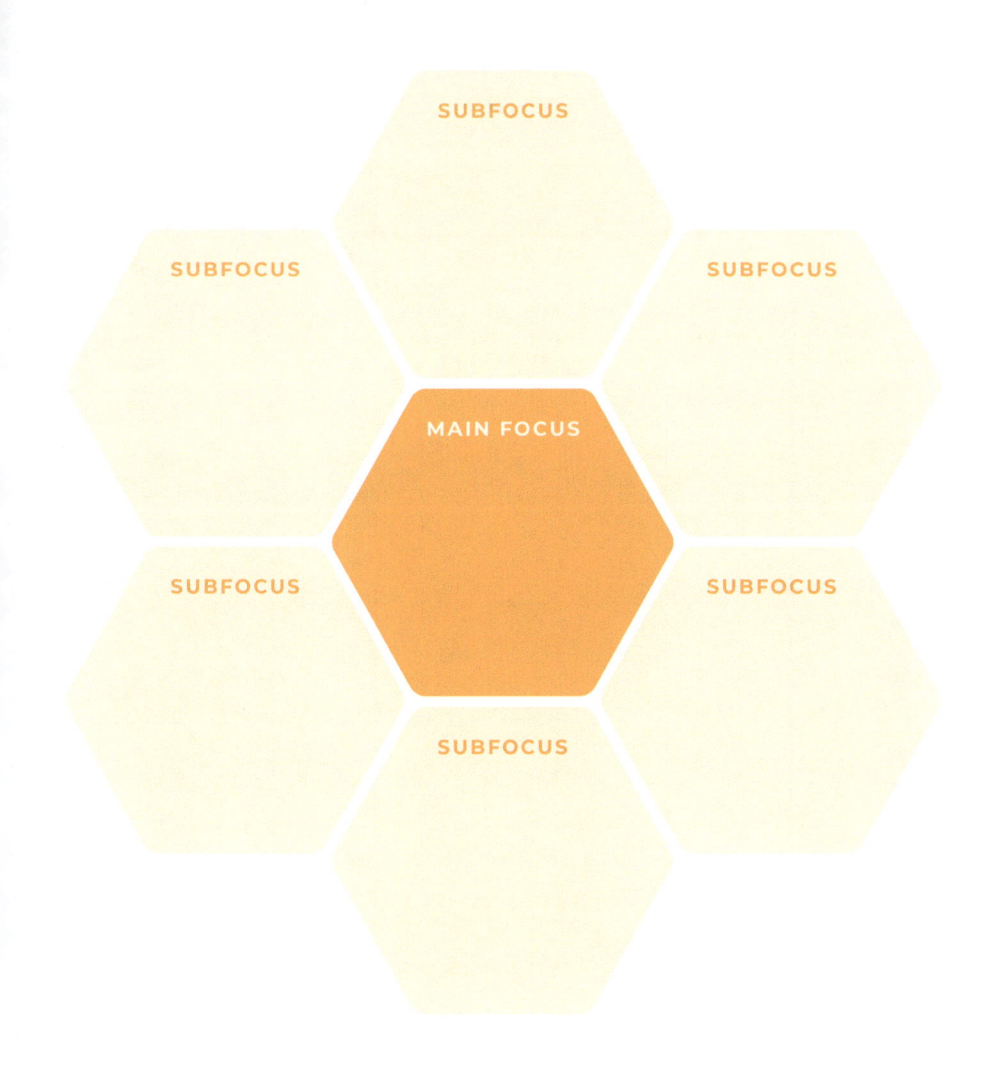

SUBFOCUS

SUBFOCUS

SUBFOCUS

SYMBOLIC	▶	INTERPRETATION	▶	
SYMBOLIC	▶	INTERPRETATION	▶	
SYMBOLIC	▶	INTERPRETATION	▶	
SYMBOLIC	▶	INTERPRETATION	▶	
SYMBOLIC	▶	INTERPRETATION	▶	
SYMBOLIC	▶	INTERPRETATION	▶	
SYMBOLIC	▶	INTERPRETATION	▶	

INTERPRETATION SUMMARY

APPLICATION

Dream Title

Dream Title

DAY OF THE WEEK

S M T W T F S

DATE

/ /

PRIMARY EMOTION

+ / −

DREAM CONTENT

Dreams work for the mind, soul, and spirit the way that kidneys work for the body. They filter information and revelation.

Dream Mapping

TYPE(S) OF DREAM *(Check all that apply)*

- Body Dream
- Soul Dream
- Demonic Dream
- God Dream

LENSES OF INTERPRETATION *(Check once completed)*

- Holy Spirit
- Emotion
- Dreamer's Personal / Cultural Experience
- Interpreter's Personal / Cultural Experience

MAIN FOCUS	▶		▶	LITERAL
SUBFOCUS	▶		▶	LITERAL
SUBFOCUS	▶		▶	LITERAL
SUBFOCUS	▶		▶	LITERAL
SUBFOCUS	▶		▶	LITERAL
SUBFOCUS	▶		▶	LITERAL
SUBFOCUS	▶		▶	LITERAL

SUBFOCUS

SUBFOCUS

SUBFOCUS

SUBFOCUS

MAIN FOCUS

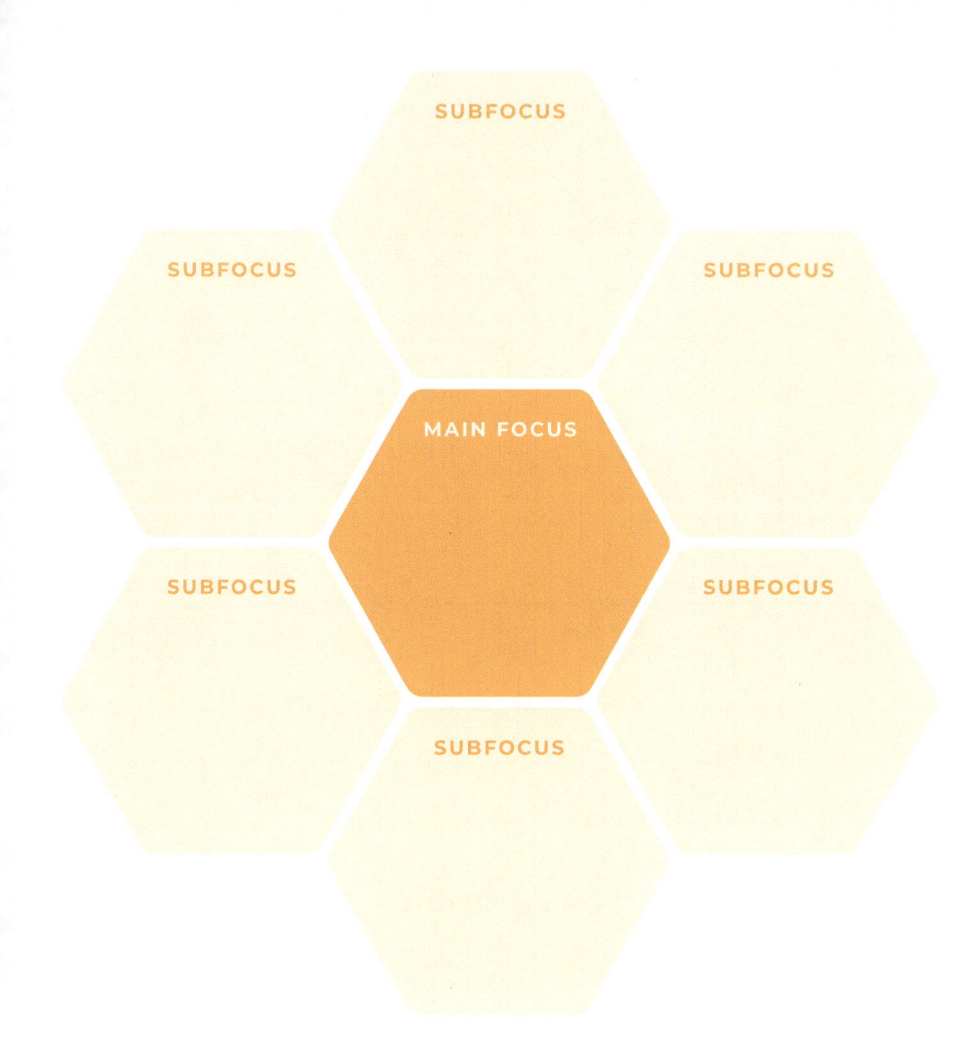

SUBFOCUS

SUBFOCUS

SUBFOCUS

SYMBOLIC	▶	INTERPRETATION	▶	
SYMBOLIC	▶	INTERPRETATION	▶	
SYMBOLIC	▶	INTERPRETATION	▶	
SYMBOLIC	▶	INTERPRETATION	▶	
SYMBOLIC	▶	INTERPRETATION	▶	
SYMBOLIC	▶	INTERPRETATION	▶	
SYMBOLIC	▶	INTERPRETATION	▶	

INTERPRETATION SUMMARY

APPLICATION

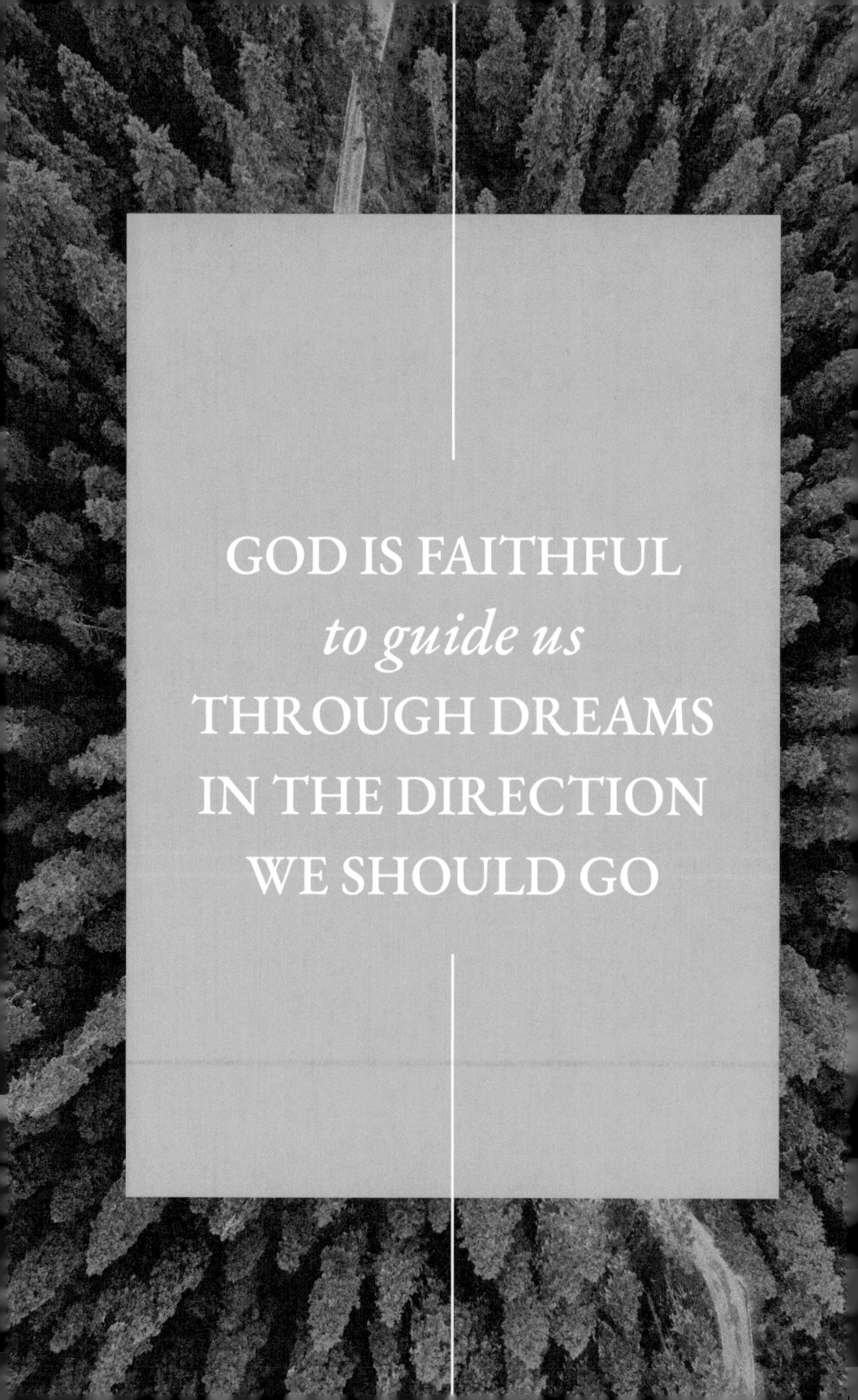

GOD IS FAITHFUL
to guide us
**THROUGH DREAMS
IN THE DIRECTION
WE SHOULD GO**

Divine Direction in Dreams

DEVOTIONAL NO. 6

And having been warned in a dream not to go back to Herod, they returned to their country by another route.

// MATTHEW 2:12 (NIV)

But when he heard that Archelaus was reigning in Judea in place of his father Herod, he was afraid to go there. Having been warned in a dream, he withdrew to the district of Galilee.

// MATTHEW 2:22 (NIV)

God can use dreams to give us direction and warnings. The first dream mentioned above saved the lives of the three Magi who visited Jesus after his birth, and the second dream warned Joseph of impending danger and protected Jesus's life. Have you ever received a warning in a dream? God is faithful to guide us through dreams in the direction we should go.

DEVOTIONAL NOTES

Dream Title

Dream Title

DAY OF THE WEEK 　　　 DATE 　　　 PRIMARY EMOTION

S　M　T　W　T　F　S　　　 / 　 / 　　　 + 　 / 　 –

DREAM CONTENT

*Mystery increases the opportunities for intimacy
because it invites us into a deeper conversation with God.*

Dream Mapping

TYPE(S) OF DREAM *(Check all that apply)*

- Body Dream
- Soul Dream
- Demonic Dream
- God Dream

LENSES OF INTERPRETATION *(Check once completed)*

- Holy Spirit
- Emotion
- Dreamer's Personal / Cultural Experience
- Interpreter's Personal / Cultural Experience

MAIN FOCUS	▶		▶	LITERAL
SUBFOCUS	▶		▶	LITERAL
SUBFOCUS	▶		▶	LITERAL
SUBFOCUS	▶		▶	LITERAL
SUBFOCUS	▶		▶	LITERAL
SUBFOCUS	▶		▶	LITERAL
SUBFOCUS	▶		▶	LITERAL

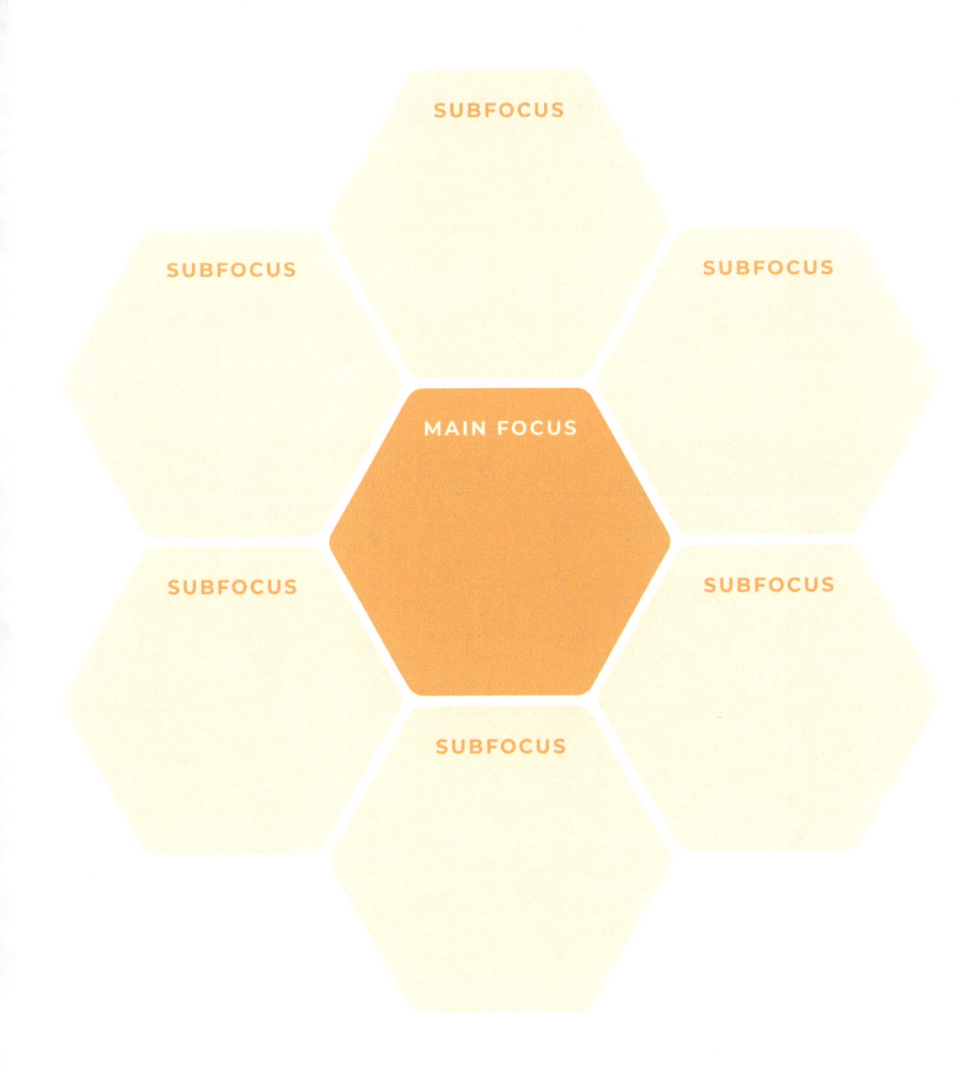

SUBFOCUS

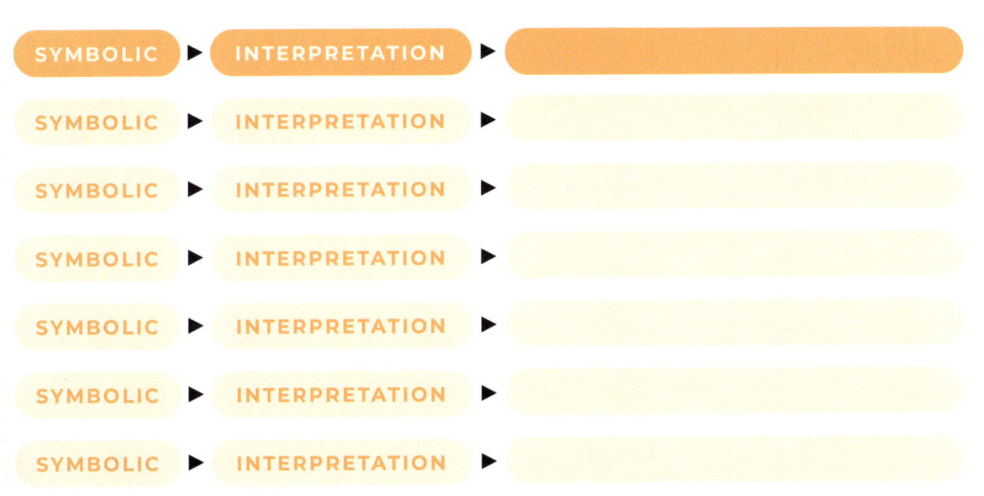

SUBFOCUS

SUBFOCUS

MAIN FOCUS

SUBFOCUS

SUBFOCUS

SUBFOCUS

SYMBOLIC	▶	INTERPRETATION	▶	
SYMBOLIC	▶	INTERPRETATION	▶	
SYMBOLIC	▶	INTERPRETATION	▶	
SYMBOLIC	▶	INTERPRETATION	▶	
SYMBOLIC	▶	INTERPRETATION	▶	
SYMBOLIC	▶	INTERPRETATION	▶	
SYMBOLIC	▶	INTERPRETATION	▶	

INTERPRETATION SUMMARY

APPLICATION

Dream Title

Dream Title

DAY OF THE WEEK
S M T W T F S

DATE
/ /

PRIMARY EMOTION
+ / −

DREAM CONTENT

*Feelings and impressions can be languages
God uses to speak to us.*

Dream Mapping

TYPE(S) OF DREAM *(Check all that apply)*

- Body Dream
- Soul Dream
- Demonic Dream
- God Dream

LENSES OF INTERPRETATION *(Check once completed)*

- Holy Spirit
- Emotion
- Dreamer's Personal / Cultural Experience
- Interpreter's Personal / Cultural Experience

MAIN FOCUS ▶	▶ LITERAL
SUBFOCUS ▶	▶ LITERAL
SUBFOCUS ▶	▶ LITERAL
SUBFOCUS ▶	▶ LITERAL
SUBFOCUS ▶	▶ LITERAL
SUBFOCUS ▶	▶ LITERAL
SUBFOCUS ▶	▶ LITERAL

SUBFOCUS

SUBFOCUS

SUBFOCUS

MAIN FOCUS

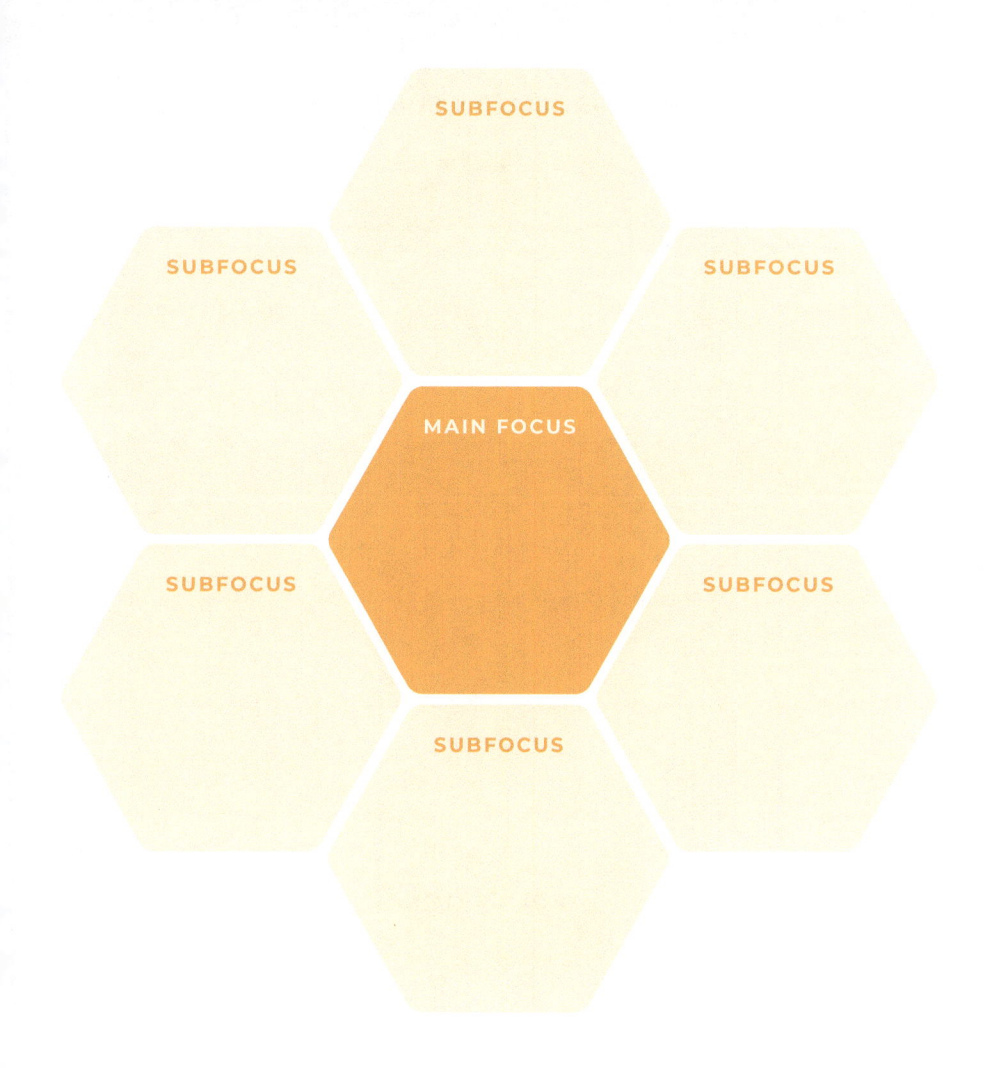

SUBFOCUS

SUBFOCUS

SUBFOCUS

SYMBOLIC	▶	INTERPRETATION	▶	
SYMBOLIC	▶	INTERPRETATION	▶	
SYMBOLIC	▶	INTERPRETATION	▶	
SYMBOLIC	▶	INTERPRETATION	▶	
SYMBOLIC	▶	INTERPRETATION	▶	
SYMBOLIC	▶	INTERPRETATION	▶	
SYMBOLIC	▶	INTERPRETATION	▶	

INTERPRETATION SUMMARY

APPLICATION

Dream Title

Dream Title

DAY OF THE WEEK
S M T W T F S

DATE
/ /

PRIMARY EMOTION
+ / −

DREAM CONTENT

The key to understanding dreams is using a combination of symbolic understanding and the ability to hear God's voice.

Dream Mapping

TYPE(S) OF DREAM *(Check all that apply)*

- ○ Body Dream
- ○ Soul Dream
- ○ Demonic Dream
- ○ God Dream

LENSES OF INTERPRETATION *(Check once completed)*

- ○ Holy Spirit
- ○ Emotion
- ○ Dreamer's Personal / Cultural Experience
- ○ Interpreter's Personal / Cultural Experience

MAIN FOCUS	▶		▶	LITERAL
SUBFOCUS	▶		▶	LITERAL
SUBFOCUS	▶		▶	LITERAL
SUBFOCUS	▶		▶	LITERAL
SUBFOCUS	▶		▶	LITERAL
SUBFOCUS	▶		▶	LITERAL
SUBFOCUS	▶		▶	LITERAL

                          SUBFOCUS

        SUBFOCUS   SUBFOCUS

                         MAIN FOCUS

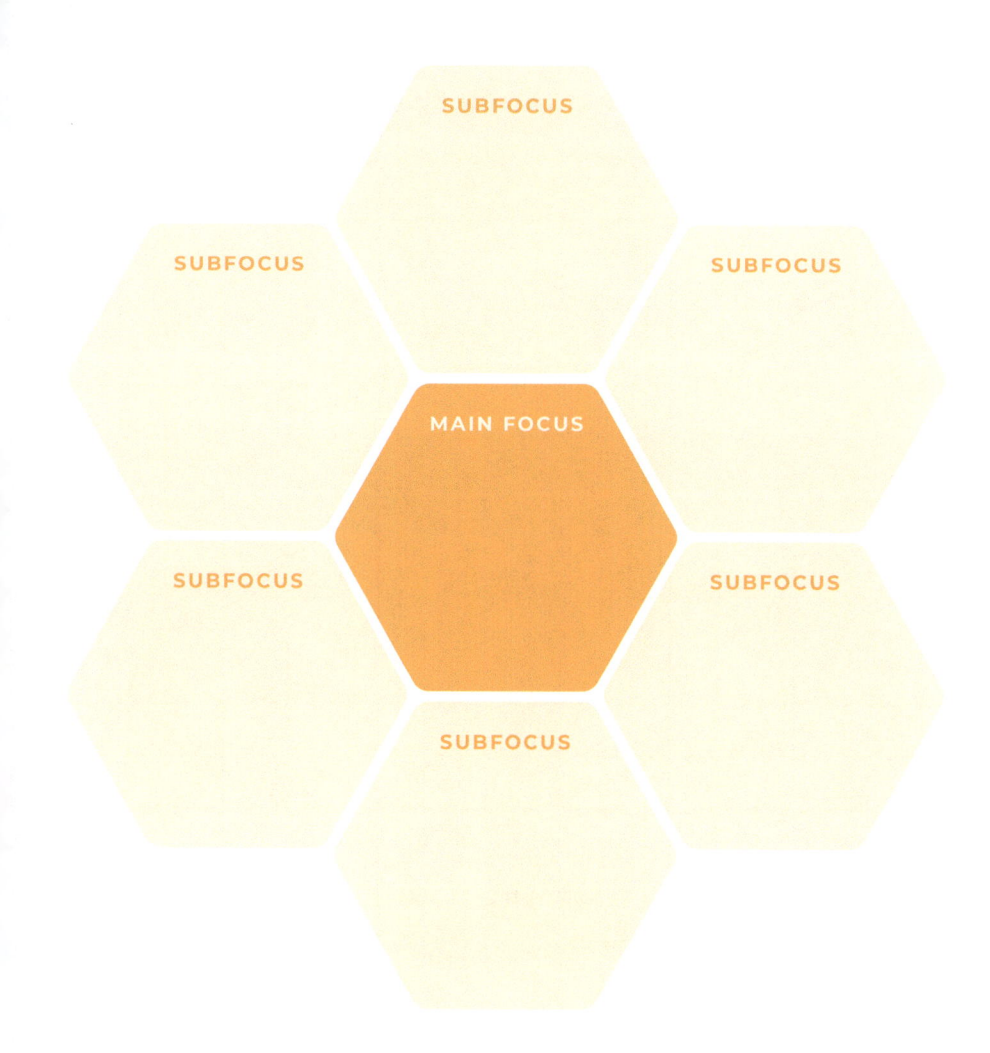

        SUBFOCUS   SUBFOCUS

                          SUBFOCUS

SYMBOLIC	▶	INTERPRETATION	▶	
SYMBOLIC	▶	INTERPRETATION	▶	
SYMBOLIC	▶	INTERPRETATION	▶	
SYMBOLIC	▶	INTERPRETATION	▶	
SYMBOLIC	▶	INTERPRETATION	▶	
SYMBOLIC	▶	INTERPRETATION	▶	
SYMBOLIC	▶	INTERPRETATION	▶	

INTERPRETATION SUMMARY

APPLICATION

Dream Title

Dream Title

DAY OF THE WEEK	DATE	PRIMARY EMOTION
S M T W T F S	/ /	+ / −

DREAM CONTENT

God releases strategies in the night.

Dream Mapping

TYPE(S) OF DREAM *(Check all that apply)*

- ○ Body Dream
- ○ Soul Dream
- ○ Demonic Dream
- ○ God Dream

LENSES OF INTERPRETATION *(Check once completed)*

- ○ Holy Spirit
- ○ Emotion
- ○ Dreamer's Personal / Cultural Experience
- ○ Interpreter's Personal / Cultural Experience

MAIN FOCUS	▶		▶	LITERAL
SUBFOCUS	▶		▶	LITERAL
SUBFOCUS	▶		▶	LITERAL
SUBFOCUS	▶		▶	LITERAL
SUBFOCUS	▶		▶	LITERAL
SUBFOCUS	▶		▶	LITERAL
SUBFOCUS	▶		▶	LITERAL

SUBFOCUS

SUBFOCUS

SUBFOCUS

SUBFOCUS

MAIN FOCUS

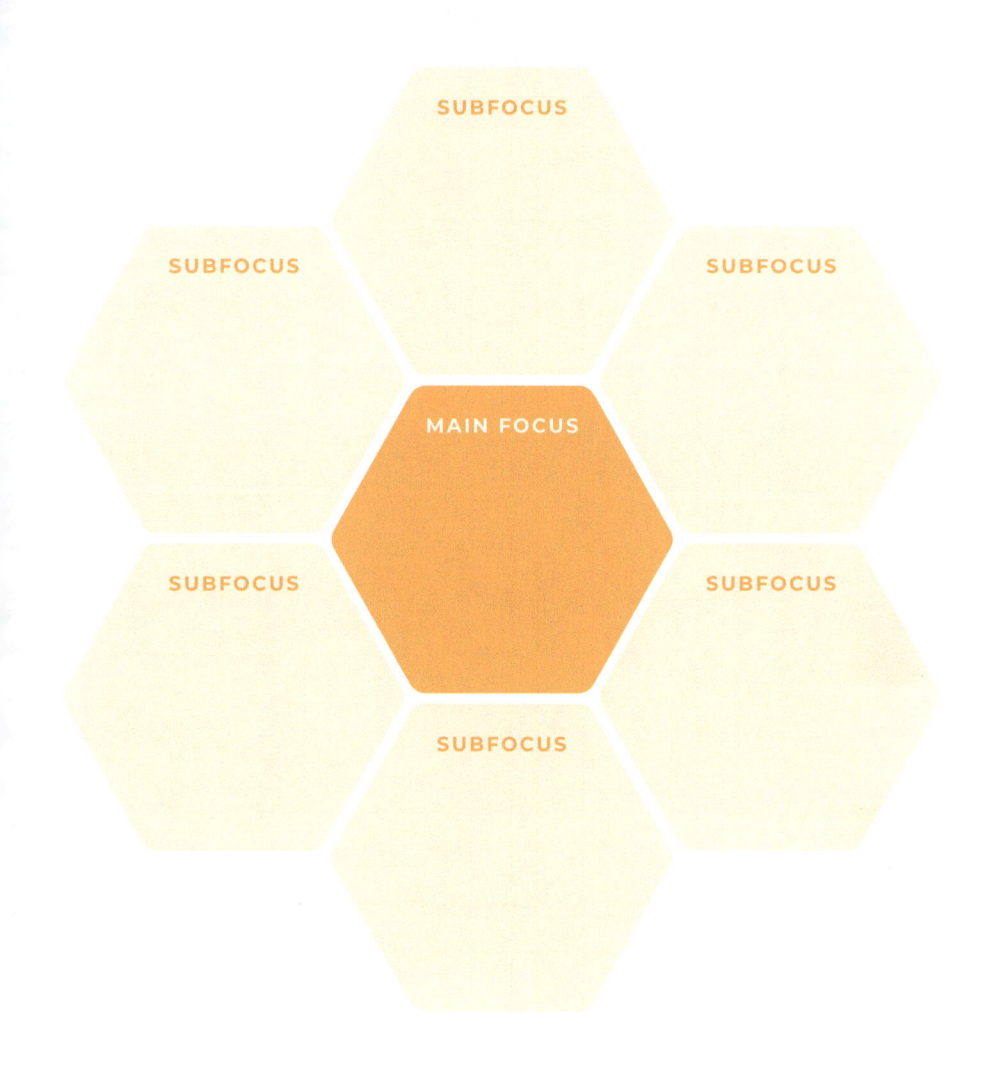

SUBFOCUS

SUBFOCUS

SUBFOCUS

SYMBOLIC	▶	INTERPRETATION	▶	
SYMBOLIC	▶	INTERPRETATION	▶	
SYMBOLIC	▶	INTERPRETATION	▶	
SYMBOLIC	▶	INTERPRETATION	▶	
SYMBOLIC	▶	INTERPRETATION	▶	
SYMBOLIC	▶	INTERPRETATION	▶	
SYMBOLIC	▶	INTERPRETATION	▶	

INTERPRETATION SUMMARY

APPLICATION

Dream Title

Dream Title

DAY OF THE WEEK   DATE   PRIMARY EMOTION

S M T W T F S   / /   + / −

DREAM CONTENT

*Keeping a childlike heart of wonder and gratitude
will make you a target for more dreams.*

Dream Mapping

TYPE(S) OF DREAM *(Check all that apply)*

- Body Dream
- Soul Dream
- Demonic Dream
- God Dream

LENSES OF INTERPRETATION *(Check once completed)*

- Holy Spirit
- Emotion
- Dreamer's Personal / Cultural Experience
- Interpreter's Personal / Cultural Experience

MAIN FOCUS ▶	▶ LITERAL
SUBFOCUS ▶	▶ LITERAL
SUBFOCUS ▶	▶ LITERAL
SUBFOCUS ▶	▶ LITERAL
SUBFOCUS ▶	▶ LITERAL
SUBFOCUS ▶	▶ LITERAL
SUBFOCUS ▶	▶ LITERAL

SUBFOCUS

SUBFOCUS

SUBFOCUS

MAIN FOCUS

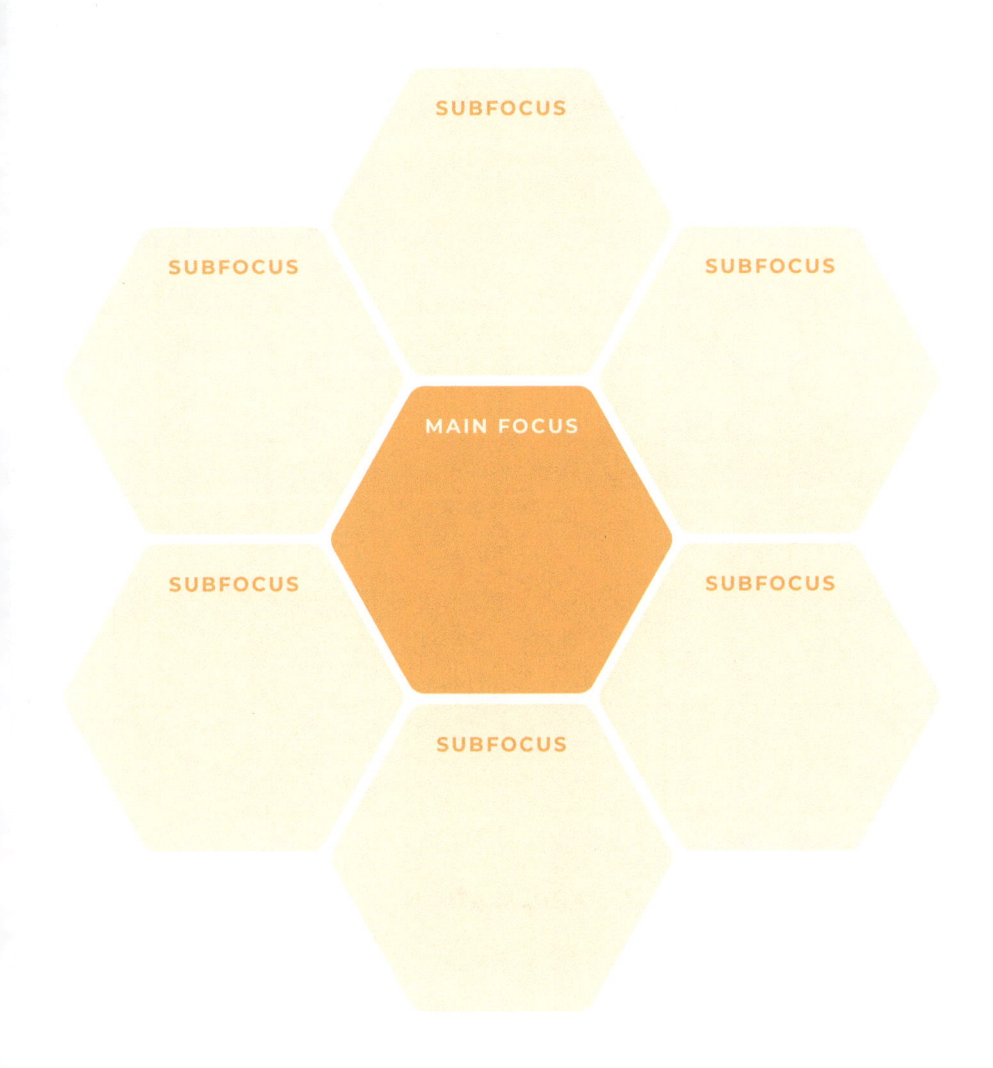

SUBFOCUS

SUBFOCUS

SUBFOCUS

SYMBOLIC	▶	INTERPRETATION	▶	
SYMBOLIC	▶	INTERPRETATION	▶	
SYMBOLIC	▶	INTERPRETATION	▶	
SYMBOLIC	▶	INTERPRETATION	▶	
SYMBOLIC	▶	INTERPRETATION	▶	
SYMBOLIC	▶	INTERPRETATION	▶	
SYMBOLIC	▶	INTERPRETATION	▶	

INTERPRETATION SUMMARY

APPLICATION

Acknowledgments

Heather, Conner, Kira, and Madison Armstrong:
MY FAMILY - HERITAGE OF DREAMERS

Kim Koch, Jamie Cherf, Lindsey Reiman, and Brady Voss:
THE DREAM TEAM - DESIGN DIRECTION AND PROJECT MANAGEMENT

Karla Dial and Marielle Spanvi:
COPY EDITING

BEN ARMSTRONG is a renowned international speaker, celebrated teacher and now author, and the overseer of Prophetic Ministries at Bethel Church in Redding, California, where he also serves on the Senior Leadership and Church Leadership teams with his wife, Heather Armstrong.

While growing up in Weaverville, California, Ben was deeply impacted and mentored by two incredible men: Geoff Armstrong and Bill Johnson. Geoff, Ben's dad, demonstrated what a loving, affectionate father looks like, and taught Ben a steadfast work ethic as well as the skills of being a general building contractor. The work ethic and love of building still drive Ben to this day; in his free time he enjoys building furniture for his family. Bill Johnson instilled in Ben a passion for living in purity and power, and giving oneself in worship, prayer, and partnership with the Holy Spirit. Through his ministry, Bill also deposited in Ben a love of nations and a sense of responsibility to sow into the Kingdom being established all over the world.

Ben's ministry is marked by wisdom and revelation. He is a true dreamer, and dreaming is a gift that has manifested in his life from a young age. He has immersed himself in a lifelong pursuit of deciphering the multifaceted ways God communicates with His children and has become adept at interpreting His voice. (As a matter of fact, Ben's middle name is Joseph—a fitting tribute to the biblical patriarch renowned for his gift of interpreting dreams.)

When he is not speaking or writing, Ben enjoys the simple pleasures of life, including spending time with Heather and their three children—Conner, Kira, and Madison. He loves building, and caring for his beloved goats and plants, and he is an avid lover of donuts.

Overall, Ben is a visionary leader whose stewardship has touched the hearts and minds of people all over the world. He continues to inspire and lead people in knowing and recognizing the heart and languages of God. One of his core beliefs is that God is present in every aspect of our lives—including our likes and dislikes. It's become his mission to help invite others into the type of revelatory and intimate partnership that he enjoys with the Holy Spirit—and that's why he loves to teach about dream interpretation.

Made in the USA
Columbia, SC
09 March 2024